Toddlers
at Play

Books by Dr. Marilyn Daniels

Dancing with Words: Signing for Hearing Children's Literacy
Benedictine Roots in the Development of Deaf Education:
Listening with the Heart
The Dance in Christianity: A History of Religious Dance through the Ages
Sign to Speak: Babies Can Talk

Books by Ken and Georgia Frawley

Sign to Speak: Babies Can Talk
Play-Along Songs: Musical Activities for Children Volume 1
Play-Along Songs: Fun Children's Activity Songs Volume 2

DVDs by We Sign

Babies and Toddlers 2
Baby Songs
Play Time
Fun Time
ABCs
Numbers
Colors
Animals
Rhymes
More Animals
Classroom Favorites
Santa's Favorite Christmas Songs
Christmas Carols
Patriotic Songs

Sign to Speak Books

Babies Can Talk

Sign to Speak
Toddlers at Play

Marilyn Daniels, PhD
Georgia Frawley, MA
Ken Frawley

PRODUCTION ASSOCIATES, INC.
Orange, California

Production Associates, Inc.
1206 W. Collins Ave.
Orange, CA 92867
www.wesign.com

Printed in the United States of America

Publisher's Cataloging-in-Publication data

Daniels, Marilyn.
   Sign to speak – toddlers at play / by Dr. Marilyn Daniels, Georgia Frawley, M.A. and Ken Frawley.
   p. cm.
   Includes bibliographical references and index.
   Series : Sign to speak ; 2
   ISBN 9781887120913

1. Nonverbal communication in children. 2. Interpersonal communication in children. 3. Child rearing. 4. Sign language. 5. American sign language. I. Frawley, Georgia. II. Frawley, Ken. III. Series. IV. Title.

BF720.C65 D36 2010
419/.7—dc22   2009920654

Executive Project Director: Mike Cash
Cover and interior design: Bryan Spencer
Photo editing: Ben Marker
Copyediting: PeopleSpeak
Signing models: Sarah Hogan and Jason Roehm
Photography: Guy Cali and Don Solo
Original rhymes and songs by Ken Frawley:
   I Went Outside One Day
   Mommy Says I Love You!
   It's Time to Go to Sleep
   Stop, Look and Listen
   One Little Kitty
   Jacob Wore a Red Hat

For my great-grandsons
Elijah John and Anthony Laurence
and all young children

Marilyn Daniels

Contents

Preface

Incorporating American Sign Language into the lives of hearing toddlers is a fun activity that has amazing benefits for both toddler and parent, and fortunately it isn't necessary to know any sign language to get started or to have started signing when your child was a baby.

For toddlers, signing is a powerful gift that, at their age and stage of development, is a very different activity than signing with a baby. Toddlers, children from about 15 months to 3 years of age, are going through an important phase of their lives. They have grown out of the baby stage and are transitioning into the preschool stage. *Sign to Speak: Toddlers at Play* focuses specifically on the abilities, requirements, and interests of children at this stage.

Signing with toddlers provides them with rich learning experiences, vocabulary, and language development and helps to foster a real enthusiasm for learning. For parents, teachers, and caregivers signing provides for not only increased communication, as it does for babies, but now it also offers parents effective and useful silent behavior controls that greatly reduce parent-toddler frustrations.

Together we have over 70 years of signing experience, and our approach is proven, practical, fun, and informative. Our "hands-on" concepts, easy-to-follow tips, playful activities, and age-specific signs require no previous signing knowledge or experience. All that you need is the desire to engage in this beneficial activity.

Many compelling reasons for parents to sign with their toddlers will be presented through the course of this book. We also believe that it is beneficial for all parents, teachers, and caregivers to know why signing works. There is information on the science and research that support signing with hearing children along with historical perspectives about American Sign Language, commonly known as ASL. This information is intended to empower readers and make them more successful in using sign language with hearing toddlers.

Acknowledgments

Since my initial research, when I first began to examine the value of ASL for hearing children, I received assistance and encouragement from the Deaf community. During the intervening years, as my research expanded to include hearing people from infancy to old age, this Deaf co-culture has consistently been open to sharing their nonverbal manual language with me. Their support began in the early 1990s in Pennsylvania at the Scranton State School for the Deaf. It was there that Deaf mothers of hearing children allowed their offspring to participate in my very first research study in this area. This support continued and took on national and international ramifications when I was invited to participate in state, regional, and national conferences of the Deaf in California, New York, New Jersey, Pennsylvania, Michigan, Maryland, South Carolina, and Utah. During the summer of 2003, I was invited to teach at Nagoya University in Nagoya, Japan. How thrilling to find the local Deaf community supportive and attending my lectures in this foreign country. The Japanese were intent in learning how educators in the United States used ASL to enhance communication and English language development in hearing populations. They were eager to understand the methods I used. My previous work with the American Deaf community was significant in this regard and recently culminated in an invitation to share my research in Calgary, Canada. At this national conference of Deaf educators the participants, both deaf and hearing, were excited to learn about the ASL techniques I wrote about and adapt them with their children and students. The Deaf community in the United States and throughout the world has remained supportive of my work for nearly 20 years. I acknowledge with gratitude their generosity and willingness to share their language, American Sign Language, with me and the rest of the hearing world.

Marilyn Daniels, PhD

Sign to Speak: Toddlers at Play is the result of the support, time, effort, and influence of many people. Among those Mike Cash, president of Production Associates, has spent countless hours directing and producing everything for this product every step of the way. Ben Marker worked for many months creating the artwork for each of the signs. Sharon Goldinger edited and guided us through the direction that this book would take. We wish to thank Bryan Spencer for the cover design and book layout, Sarah Hogan and Jason Roehm for being our signing models and Don Solo and Guy Cali for photography. We also want to acknowledge the great pleasure it has been to work with Marilyn Daniels, a true professional and kindred spirit.

Ken and Georgia Frawley

Introduction

As your child grows, you will suddenly find yourself the parent of a toddler. Toddlers, children from about 15 months to 3 years old, are going through a new and important phase in their lives. They have outgrown the baby stage and are growing into the preschool stage. Their use of language is expanding, if not exploding. Their abilities, needs, and interests are very different from those of babies and older children. That's why this book focuses specifically on this stage of childhood.

Using American Sign Language (ASL) with hearing toddlers gives them a playful way to expand their vocabularies and enhance their use of language. When parents, teachers, and caregivers sign with toddlers, they encourage learning and help these children develop an enthusiasm for knowledge that can last a lifetime.

Sometimes parents, who have been signing with their babies, believe that they should stop once spoken language begins. This is a mistake. Absolutely no evidence suggests that using sign language interferes in any way with a child's use of English, but plenty of evidence shows that signing provides rich rewards for both parent and child and enhances their literacy.

On the other hand, you may think that it's too late to start signing with your children once they become toddlers. This is also a mistake. Toddlers naturally enjoy signing, and you and your child can reap many benefits by engaging in this fun activity.

What are some of those benefits? First, signing allows parents to shape the behavior of toddlers as they fearlessly explore their world—without ever raising your voice. Second, signing allows toddlers to have up to twice the usable vocabulary of nonsigning children, including words that they cannot say yet. Imagine how wonderful it will be if your toddlers can tell you what they want or need without a tantrum.

This book will introduce parents, teachers and caregivers of toddlers to techniques, tips, practical signs, and activities that will make everyone successful with signing. No previous knowledge of American Sign Language is required. You just need the desire and enthusiasm to bring signing into the lives of children for learning and playful interactive activities.

Toddlers who can sign are well on their way to acquiring a second modern language in addition to English. For children in bilingual homes, ASL becomes a third language in their communication toolbox.

How This Book Came About

Dr. Marilyn Daniels's interest grew out of her interactions with some of her graduate students in a communication theories course. Many of the students made extra money serving as sign language interpreters for hearing children of Deaf parents. They would often attend parent-teacher conferences at elementary schools and interpret the teachers' comments for the Deaf parents. The graduate students were surprised to learn that these schoolchildren were doing extremely well in all of their language arts classes. "Why would this be the case?" they asked. These children came from homes where little or no English was spoken, and they had all learned ASL as their first language. The students said, "It doesn't make sense."

Marilyn tended to agree with them and had no good explanation for this. But her interest was piqued, and she began to delve more deeply into the puzzle. Corroborating interviews with interpreters in Pennsylvania, New Jersey, and Connecticut who worked with hearing children of Deaf parents indicated that this was not an isolated phenomenon. Armed with that knowledge, she decided to do her own research.

Her first study, "ASL as a Factor in Acquiring English," was published in *Sign Language Studies* in 1993. This research examined the size of the vocabularies of 14 hearing children in Pennsylvania ranging in age from 2 years, 10 months to 13 years, 6 months. The children all had normal hearing. They had learned ASL as babies and were fluent in both ASL and English. With the exception of one child, who was the daughter of an interpreter, they all had one or more Deaf parents.

Their vocabularies were measured with the Peabody Vocabulary Test. This is a well-respected test of receptive English vocabulary that has been used by educators in its successive editions for more than 50 years. Because this test's outcomes are age referenced, it can be administered to anyone between the ages of 2 years, 6 months and 40. The expected score for someone with an average vocabulary is 100. The mean derived score of the 14 children was 109.57, significantly higher than scores expected from a randomly selected sample. This result clearly demonstrated that children who learned ASL as babies acquired a far larger English vocabulary than would be expected of typical children.

These results were very exciting because they indicated that knowing ASL offered strong language and literacy benefits to hearing youngsters. The "wow" factor of these numbers catapulted Marilyn into doing further research. She began a quest to discover whether similar results would occur in different populations with other babies and young children.

Now, years later, and after countless hours of research, the results of her efforts have demonstrated that ASL offers a myriad of educational advantages to children ranging in age from infancy through age 13. All of Marilyn's interactions with parents, grandparents, teachers, and the beneficiaries of this ongoing effort, the babies and children who have learned ASL, have led her to the view that ASL is an almost magical approach for language learning. Her book *Dancing with Words: Signing for Hearing Children's Literacy* has become one of the most widely used and quoted resources for signing with children of all ages.

Memory and recall, early communication, language development, and frustration reduction through the use of American Sign Language were things Georgia Frawley had been aware of for years. She first encountered the use of ASL with children when she worked as a dorm counselor at the California School for the Deaf in Riverside. This was an amazing experience for her: in one day she easily went from knowing no signs to knowing more than 30.

Years later, she used the signs she had learned at the School for the Deaf, in combination with speaking, as her way to communicate with her own infants. She believed that signing was a simple way to reinforce language development. However, when her children began signing words when they were as young as 8 months old, she realized that signing provided them with a language skill. This allowed her children to tell her what they wanted without crying or screaming.

Georgia has been teaching high school classes in Child Development for over 30 years. During her career, she taught Careers with Children classes. There she prepared students to work with young children. Included in the curriculum were theories by renowned psychologists Erik Erikson, Abraham Maslow, and Howard Gardner. They all agree that when working with children, a caregiver needs to focus on the children 's developmental stages, always meet their needs, include as many learning opportunities as possible, and encourage children to maximize their learning potential. Georgia has found that signing, especially when incorporated with music, is a surefire way to engage children and enable all children to be successful.

Georgia also developed and supervised an on-campus day-care center at her high school and worked closely with various day-care centers and preschools in her area. Her day-care parents and Child Development students cared for children ranging in age from 6 weeks to 4 years old. Signing with these children became part of the routine. Over the years she has heard many positive stories and comments about the use of signing with young children.

Ken Frawley graduated from college with the intention of becoming an elementary school teacher in California. He began to perform music and storytelling programs for children in preschools, in elementary schools, at libraries, and at various other community events. After one of his concerts, a signing friend said, "It would be nice if Deaf and hearing children had something they could do together." Ken decided to add singing and signing to his concerts.

To his amazement, he found that children remembered many of the signs he had shown them, even a year later. After a little bit of research, it became very clear to Ken that we all learn and remember better when we are involved in what we are being taught. As we have known for thousands of years, learning that involves a variety of our senses is a powerful memory and recall tool. Sign language and songs engage children visually and verbally, through movement, music, and more.

In the early 1990s Ken cofounded Production Associates and began producing ASL products for children of all ages. The products he helped produce were designed to provide members of each age group with a fun way to include ASL in their lives while learning and remembering a lot of vocabulary and educational concepts. All the titles he helped to create were designed to be interactive and to provide clear instruction for parents, teachers, and caregivers so that they could engage in this activity with their children and keep the visual images fun and interesting.

Ken helped design the original Say, Sing and Sign video series, which later became the We Sign series featuring ASL for hearing children, teachers, and families. Ken and Georgia were two of the pioneers in the field of signing for hearing children. They began by providing preschool and elementary school children with videos and DVDs of songs and signs for learning the basics: *ABC, Numbers, Colors, Rhymes,* and *Animals.* Eventually, they changed the series name to We Sign and added the *Babies & Toddlers* DVD so parents could learn to use signs for early communication and learning. Finally they joined Dr. Marilyn Daniels to write their first book, *Sign to Speak: Babies Can Talk.*

For years, Ken and Georgia have worked hard to educate the country on the benefits of signing for hearing children. They have lectured and taught parents, educators, and caregivers across the United States the We Sign concepts about signing with children. As part of the We Sign team, they have coauthored this book in an effort to continue empowering parents, teachers, caregivers, and children not only with the foundation for developing language skills and a way to ease communication frustrations but also with a playful way to support early learning and language growth.

The authors have received positive reactions and accolades from parents, teachers, and caregivers about the use of signing with all children. They wanted to develop a signing book that was specifically targeted to toddlers and their needs, interests, and developmental abilities while providing a manual language for early communication, learning, and fun. They hope that by engaging in signing with toddlers, parents, and educators will become as enthusiastic as the authors are and experience the educational advantages outlined in this book.

How to Get the Most from This Book

This book is broken into three parts and an appendix. Part 1 offers the research on why signing works and an explanation for why we recommend using ASL rather than made-up gestures.

Part 2 allows you to start signing right away. The "Jump Start on Smart" offers you signs that we have found to be the most effective with toddlers in our many years of experience with parents, teachers, and caregivers, along with simple tips for successful signing with your toddler.

Part 3 offers playful and interactive signing activities that you and your toddler will love. Here you will learn how to incorporate signing into walks, with singing songs and rhymes, telling stories, reading books, and playing games. You can learn to put together a signing journal that will allow you to look back over the years at the fun signs and activities you and your toddler engaged in.

Each of these lively activities supports your toddler's language development and gives you ways to make signing a fun part of your daily life. Our instructions in this section are often between one parent and one child. Teachers and caregivers can easily use and adapt the information and the structure to include multiple children into the activity. Just engage each toddler in the activity and encourage them all to participate.

Finally, the Toddlers at Play Toolbox in the appendix offers an alphabetical glossary of all the signs in this book, quick-reference pages on the manual alphabet, signs for numbers 1 to 10, and signs of popular colors and pages featuring 12 everyday signs for toddlers. The quick-reference pages are ideal for you to copy for your personal use and give to family members and caregivers so that they can sign with your child too. You'll find useful signing resources, free materials, music downloads, and video demonstrations at www.signtospeak.com.

This book can be used along with the *We Sign: Babies & Toddlers* DVD, which features signs, instruction, tips, and a visual dictionary. It's one of We Sign's award-winning DVDs with which you and your child can grow. You can also download the songs and rhymes in the book through iTunes. Visit www.signtospeak.com and use the log-in code STST109A to access the downloads and information.

No matter how you decide to explore this book, we believe you will find signing with your toddler to be a fun and rewarding adventure, one that you will want to continue as your child moves into preschool, elementary school, and beyond.

PART I

All about Using ASL with Toddlers

Chapter 1
Why Sign with Your Toddler?

Parents often ask, "Should I continue to sign now that my child has started to talk?" Or conversely, they may wonder, "If my child is already a toddler, is it too late to start signing?"

If you and your toddler are already communicating with sign language, you undoubtedly have seen some of the many benefits of using signs. However, you may think ASL signs are like training wheels, and once a child starts to speak, it is time to leave them behind. This is not the case. Signs can be a lifelong addition to your child's communication toolbox.

If you have not previously used sign language with your child, this is a great time to begin. Toddlers readily take to this new way of communicating. They find the movement of signing to be fun and a challenge with which they can be successful. They will not lose their ability or desire to talk. There is absolutely no evidence, either from academic researchers or from parents and teachers, that learning sign language interferes with a child's use of English. If you start learning now, you and your toddler will soon be reaping the rewards of signing together.

The Benefits of Signing with Toddlers

Signing with toddlers has many potential benefits.

- They will develop a larger vocabulary of words they can use and can understand.
- Their emotional well-being will increase as their emotional intelligence grows by connecting signs to words and feelings.
- They can use sign to express themselves in kind and appropriate ways.
- Their behavior will be easier to manage, and they will have far fewer tantrums characteristic of the "terrible twos."
- They will be happy and engaged because they can communicate at a very young age.

These benefits are merely the beginning. Whether you are a parent who embarks on a signing adventure with your toddler for the first time or a parent who has been signing with your child since babyhood, you should experience all of these rewards. In addition, you and your toddler will enjoy the adventure and build stronger bonds as you share this language together.

Language and Vocabulary Development

It has become clear to parents, teachers, and caregivers alike that hearing children who are exposed to ASL make connections between spoken language and the visual pictures of signs. This simultaneous use of a manual language and an oral language offers toddlers an easier access to word meanings. This provides them with a larger vocabulary of usable words to clearly and effectively express themselves and understand their world.

ASL and Hearing Children

The use of ASL with hearing children has been growing since the 1970s, when linguists came to understand that ASL is a true natural language with the same linguistic features as an oral language. Many of the early studies compared signs with spoken words. These carefully controlled, systematic inquiries showed that hearing children who were exposed to sign language used and understood about 50 signs by the time they were a year old, while most children of that age who had not been exposed to sign language used and understood only about 10 English words.[1]

Additional significant studies in the 1970s and 1980s by Wilbur and Jones and P. M. Prinz and E. A. Prinz looked at the simultaneous acquisition of ASL and English by hearing children. Each of these early studies demonstrated that children exposed to both ASL and English could use the signed manual language before they used the oral language.[2] The children were able to switch easily between the two languages, and they attained a larger vocabulary of English words than typical children of comparable ages. The researchers concluded that ASL was responsible for the children's advanced English ability.

For over 30 years, a dramatically increasing number of parents and teachers have been using sign language with hearing children and have been both surprised and exceedingly pleased with the results. What began for parents who were interpreters or just familiar with American Sign Language as a natural way to speak (signing and saying words at the same time) has become an activity of which most parents are aware. This is not only due to the publicity that signing with hearing children has received and the science behind it but also to the countless testimonials that demonstrate real-world experiences.

Signing Success Story

Several years ago a local mother took her twin boys to the Norma Gray Early Learning Center in Huntington, West Virginia. The children were deaf, but their mother did not want them to be isolated from other children their own age. The day-care center's staff tried to integrate the twins with the other children, but it was difficult because the boys only used sign language. To deal with this situation, the staff members began teaching themselves American Sign Language. They then proceeded to teach ASL words to the hearing students. The director said, "We didn't want to single them out, and we wanted other children to be able to communicate with them."[3]

All of the hearing children picked up the signs so quickly that the center decided to hire a professional to develop the staff's overall signing skills. The young students appeared to be thrilled that they could communicate with signs. According to the director, the children's eyes would light up when they signed or when a teacher signed to them, and they were much more attentive. Parents started calling the school to express their delight with their children's literacy progress. The center continues to use sign language with children even when no hearing-impaired students are enrolled. This is partly so teachers will not forget the sign language, but mainly because the school staff finds it so useful.[4]

ASL Encourages a Larger Vocabulary

Parents who use sign language with their children as well as teachers in early childhood education report that children acquire a large expressive English vocabulary in addition to learning how to sign. Expressive vocabulary means the inventory of words a child uses to communicate. All evidence shows that the use of sign language typically increases a child's expressive English vocabulary by 20 to 30 percent.

Receptive vocabulary refers to the ability of children to understand the words they hear. Using both ASL and English with your toddler not only increases the ability to use more words but also allows your child to understand more words. One of the primary reasons for this result is the iconic nature of many signs. That is, the signs look like the words they represent. For example, the sign for DRINK looks like someone sipping from a cup. Signs like these offer toddlers a picture placed in the air to connect with the word the speaker is pronouncing. Looking at the picture helps children understand the meaning of the sounds being said.

DRINK—Shape your hand as if you are holding a glass then bring it up to your mouth and tip it toward you so that it looks as if you're drinking from that glass.

Children learning their first language can be compared to adults who have traveled to a foreign country and are trying to understand a foreign language. For example, if you were in Paris and someone held out a book and said *livre,* you would probably understand the French word. Likewise, if someone pointed to a door and said *porte,* you would undoubtedly understand the French word. In the same way, seeing a "moving picture" of a word provides an important clue that helps a toddler understand the meaning of a spoken word. A large amount of evidence shows that signing a word while you speak it will enhance your child's ability to comprehend and retain its meaning.

Signing a word gives your child a picture of the word as the word is spoken, and unlike hearing a word being pronounced, seeing a sign involves the visual cortex of the brain. When signing, you enhance your child's ability to understand a word by seeing and hearing it.

Babies learn with their hands and eyes before they begin to learn with their ears. By the time they are toddlers, they have accumulated a good deal of experience and are quite adept at learning with their hands and eyes. A multitude of synapses have formed in their brains and they have created a good deal of memory by using their senses of touch and sight.

Visual Learning

Many children are visual learners and signing and simultaneously speaking plays right into such children's strengths. One of the first educational researchers to acknowledge the many different ways children learn was Howard Gardner. In the 1960s he came up with his famous theory of Multiple Intelligences. Gardner put little store in standard intelligence testing. According to his Multiple Intelligences theory every individual has a variety of intelligences or ways of learning that will be discussed in detail in the next chapter. Each of the eight intelligences is independent of the others for the most part and Gardner believes every child has all of them, but no two children have exactly the same profile of intelligences.

Over the years Gardner's views have evolved and changed significantly. However, in the 1993 version of Multiple Intelligences, Gardner continues to stress the value of exposing a child to a variety of learning methods. His writings suggest he would approve of using American Sign Language as a method to help children clarify the meaning of oral words. In *The Unschooled Mind* he wrote, "Naming and classifying are central aspects of language. The capacity to name objects opens up an entire universe of meaning to the young child. Once it has come into place it is an indispensable cognitive tool."[5]

A substantial amount of evidence shows that signing a word while you speak it will enhance the ability of children to comprehend the meaning of it and retain it within their vocabularies. Signing and speaking provides a child with a larger receptive English vocabulary and a better ability to name and classify objects.

The Peabody Picture Vocabulary Test is often used to assess the vocabularies of toddlers. In this test they are shown a series of large pictures that are divided into four quadrants, and each quadrant contains a picture of a different object. The person conducting the evaluation pronounces the name of one of the four objects. The child is asked to point to the picture of the word. It is quite amazing to see the toddlers who have experienced simultaneous signing and speaking point to the correct picture with confidence and accuracy. Toddlers assessed in this manner usually have a 15 to 20 percent larger receptive English vocabulary than is expected of typical hearing children of the same age who have not been exposed to any sign language.

Bilingual Families

If your family is already bilingual, you can add sign language to the two oral languages in your home. Donavon, for example, was exposed to English, Spanish, and ASL from the time he was a baby. His mother used English and sign language with him, and his father spoke Spanish to him. He acquired an astonishingly large vocabulary in both spoken languages as well as ASL. His mother had decorated his room with alphabet strips that showed the English alphabet letters, the corresponding American manual alphabet letters, and pictures and signs representing the sounds of the letters. Donavon learned how to form the letters of the manual alphabet from these alphabet strips. He taught the children in his preschool both the signs and the Spanish words for the English words they were using in class. He began to read when he was three, and could read quite well at four. Now in middle school, Donavon has continued to excel in reading and other subjects.

Another example is three-year-old Helena. Her mother is Chinese and her father is American but speaks Chinese well. Helena's parents have been using ASL, English, and Chinese to communicate with her, and she is articulate in each language. She easily switches from English to Chinese, depending on whether she is speaking to her mother or her father.

Now that she's a toddler, Helena is interacting with many other people besides her parents. She responds to others in the language they use with her. Helena continues to use her ASL signs, and her mother and father believe her knowledge of sign language will provide her with valuable assistance as she begins to read.

Emotional Development

Signing not only helps toddlers have a larger collection of usable words, an important predictor of future reading readiness, but it also helps them to develop their emotional well-being and their emotional intelligence. A toddler's emotional intelligence will ease many of the frustrations they feel during this stage of development. Emotional intelligence, as you will learn, is another very important aspect of a toddler's future success. Signs and words used simultaneously to express feelings, give toddlers the ability to better understand their feelings, express their feelings and act in an appropriate manner.

Emotional Well-Being

Signing with toddlers can be a first step in shaping their emotional well-being because it will help you establish better communication with them. Why? Because you will be able to understand what they need and want more easily. When toddlers rely only on spoken words to communicate, they have a hard time communicating fully. However, if they have the ability to use both sign language and English, they will have a much better chance of successfully conveying their messages.

This heightened communication occurs because they have a larger expressive vocabulary, as well as a larger receptive vocabulary. Both of these strengths are necessary for a child's future literacy and academic development, but they are even more important for a toddler's emotional well-being. Being able to communicate fully gives toddlers the comfort and security of knowing that they are connected to their parents or caregivers. All human beings, no matter how young, have an innate desire to be truly connected to others and to be able to communicate with them.

Emotional Intelligence

Since the mid-1990s, we have learned much more about the mechanics of emotion. Daniel Goleman's groundbreaking book *Emotional Intelligence* is filled with scientific studies of emotion. Such investigations are possible because of the many new brain-imaging technologies that allow researchers to see glimpses of the brain at work. Suddenly, areas that were mysteries are being revealed. Neurobiological data clearly show how the brain's center for emotion can move human beings to rage, pleasure, or sorrow. Surprisingly, much of the current scientific research on the workings of emotions is being conducted with babies and young children.

The mapping of emotions widens our view of intelligence, according to Goleman. No longer is IQ considered the most important indicator of a child's destiny in life. Instead, Goleman argues, emotional intelligence is what governs a child's future.[6] He believes that children's capacity for self-control, zeal, and persistence will affect their actions and, in turn, shape their lives.

Emotion is triggered by an impulse: a feeling eager to express itself in action. Young children who lack the ability to recognize their emotions and control their actions are at the mercy of their impulses.

Emotional intelligence is a term that is currently being applied to children as young as 3 months of age. Pediatricians have begun to consider emotional milestones that children should attain at specific ages, and they are screening for these milestones in the same manner that they screen children for physical milestones such as sitting, crawling, standing, walking, running, and skipping.

Many of the attributes that doctors now look for were previously thought to be absent in babies and toddlers. Brain-imaging advances such as functional MRIs, PET scans, EEGs, and laser eye-tracking devices have shown us that babies and toddlers are much more aware of the world than psychologists once thought. For example, we now understand that babies are born with the capacity to experience both fear and contentment.

The earliest emotional markers that doctors look for in infants include deliberate responses to the people around them and the ability to engage others with a smile. By the time babies are 5 to 6 months old, they usually display emotions like surprise, joy, and frustration. When babies are 10 months old, they begin to follow their parents' gazes in an effort to understand what their parents are interested in. Gaze following is a significant ability in the early development of a child, and sign language encourages it. It is an early marker that predicts later language growth and future academic achievement.

Toddlers become more self-aware when they begin to experience complex emotions such as pride and defiance. This milestone is probably one that most parents are familiar with. Children's actions in response to these emotions often occur during the period referred to as the "terrible twos."

Understanding Feelings

Now that you understand more about the ability of very young children to experience complex emotions, you can see that it is important to help them identify their feelings and shape an emotionally intelligent response. Just because children have these feelings does not mean they can identify them, understand them, or most importantly, respond to them with appropriate behavior.

Neurological data suggest that parents have a window of opportunity for shaping their child's habits during a critical period in their toddler's life. During this period, parents can help their children modify their responses by coaching them. Helping toddlers identify feelings is the first step toward modifying their behavior, and this is much easier if you are using sign language. Through the process of signing, you are already forming a close bond with your toddler. In chapter 6 you will find many more signs for emotions.

Teaching your toddler the feeling signs one by one and discussing what each sign signifies is useful because as you identify and explore the signs, you can discuss the feelings as well. This will be helpful when your child displays a feeling, and you can say, "It looks to me like you feel sad" and make the sign for SAD. You can then discuss why the toddler is sad. You can use both words and signs as you further engage your child in a conversation about how they feel and why.

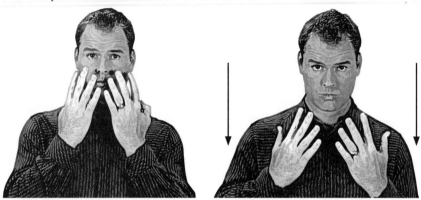

SAD—Hold your hands flat, fingers spread and palms facing in, at eye level and then move them down a little. Use with a sad facial expression.

Toddlers who attempt to recognize and understand their feelings and tie these feelings to words, both orally and manually, have taken a significant step in gaining emotional maturity. When you help your toddler name and examine their feelings and reactions to the events in their life, you will put them on a lifelong path toward wellness. During a signed and spoken conversation with toddlers, you will often discover what is truly making them sad and be able to help them figure out a solution.

Shaping Behavior

Toddlers are trying to become independent, and at the same time they are reaching out to hold a parent's or a caregiver's hand. Toddlers love to experiment. They want to strike out on their own and achieve their own accomplishments. Most have little fear and no knowledge of danger. An active toddler requires a good deal of supervision. As a result, many clashes may erupt throughout an ordinary day as you say NO over and over, and your child responds with tears. Sign language can be a balm that you use to soothe your toddler.

Signing directions like STOP or GENTLE are so much nicer, quieter, and calmer than constantly saying no, which often turns into a shouting match even when you have the best intentions. Other signs that are helpful to use with toddlers are HELP and GOOD and will be introduced in chapter 4. A very successful technique is to say and sign the instruction word and teach your toddler to respond by signing it back to you.

Signing Success Story

Signing has benefits that last far into the future. A woman in the United Kingdom recently wrote to Marilyn. This "mum" (as she described herself) had been using British Sign Language (BSL) with her daughter since she was a baby. The girl is now in her early teens, and her mum was upset with some of her daughter's friends and their risky behavior.

After she thought about the situation, she sat down with her daughter and talked about her concerns and fears, explaining how much she loved her daughter and how all she had ever wanted was for her daughter to have a healthy, happy life. She expressed her concerns and feelings about her daughter's behavior, using a good deal of BSL. During the conversation, the signs that she and her daughter had shared together over the years became more than just a mode of communication. For the daughter, they triggered a memory of the early bond she had with her mum.

The signed conversation had the desired effect. The girl's behavior changed, and the earlier bond between mum and daughter was renewed.

This mother shared her story because she believes it is important for other parents to understand the far-reaching effects that signing with your children can provide in the years following their childhood. Such benefits are not necessarily academic. Signing with children as they mature can reestablish shared communication when spoken words fail.

Conclusion

It is impossible to identify the single best reason for parents to use ASL with their toddlers because signing has so many important benefits that work together for children.

Toddlers will acquire larger expressive English vocabularies of words they can use and larger receptive English vocabularies of words they can understand. Both vocabularies are important predictors of future reading readiness. Toddlers who use and understand the signs of ASL will typically develop a healthy emotional well-being and display emotional intelligence as they interact with others. They will more readily understand their feelings and will be more likely to express these feelings in a kind and appropriate manner. Toddlers who sign appear happy and engaged. This benefit undoubtedly occurs because they are seldom frustrated; they have the ability to easily communicate their wants and desires at a very young age.

Signing with your toddler will help you establish a finer quality of communication between the two of you. This will come about because you will be able to understand what your toddler needs and wants with a stronger degree of certainty. Your toddler will be able to express these desires with signs and words used simultaneously, acting as a powerful duo. When toddlers rely only on spoken words to communicate with you, there is little chance that they will be able to fully communicate. However, if they have the ability to use both sign language and English together, the odds that they will be successful communicators is much improved.

Chapter 2
Research Supports Signing with All Children

A great deal of research shows why signing with toddlers will offer multiple benefits such as fostering earlier acquisition and more articulate spoken English communication. Emotional intelligence is the essential foundation for all learning, but several other components such as self-control and empathy are also relevant to your child's healthy development. An understanding of how your child's brain is developing can be helpful as you raise your child. The fascinating subject of memory, both long-term and short-term, and the structure and function of the brain and pertinent information about the manner in which the brain relates to the manual language of signs reveal how important signing can be to your child's development. Information about Howard Gardner's theory of Multiple Intelligences and its relevance will help you understand the value of signing with young children. Two of the interesting areas he writes about are symbols or objects and flow. Some background information will provide a framework on which to build your understanding of and commitment to signing with your toddler.

Multiple Intelligences

In the 1960s a group of academics came together at the Harvard Graduate School of Education and formed Project Zero to research human cognitive development and the process of learning. Howard Gardner was one of the original members of this endeavor. He continues to be affiliated with Project Zero through his research and now serves as the head of its steering committee. Gardner's famous theory of Multiple Intelligences was largely a result of his work with the Project Zero group.

When Gardner began his endeavors, his research goal was to discover how the mind works. He came to believe that the human mind has a set of independent computers, each assigned to a particular intelligence. In his earliest writings on the topic he named these intelligences:

- **linguistic intelligence (verbal)**—learning through speaking and listening
- **logical mathematical intelligence**—learning through logic and reason
- **musical intelligence**—learning through music, songs, rhythms, and melodies
- **spatial intelligence (visual)**—learning through seeing and reading
- **bodily-kinesthetic intelligence (physical)**—learning through movement
- **interpersonal intelligence**—learning with others
- **intrapersonal intelligence**—individual learning
- **naturalist intelligence**—learning through the environment
- **existential intelligence**—learning through reflective thinking

He was not sure about the last two intelligences so he wrote that there were at least eight and one-half intelligences.

Gardner believed each of these intelligences worked independently from the others. He assumed everyone possessed all of the intelligences. Further, he was certain that no two people had the same profile of intelligences. He found public schools in the United States were focusing on the first two intelligences, linguistic and logical mathematical, and in large measure ignoring the other intelligences. According to Gardner, this was a mistake as the intelligences being ignored were the best ways to engage some children.

During the 1980s and early 1990s he initiated programs in schools that were designed to broaden their curriculum offerings. In this way he attempted to introduce materials that would appeal to the preferred intelligences of a larger number of students. This proved to be a daunting task as there were many mandatory educational expectations as well as local, state, and federal requirements.

In Gardner's more recent writings he revisits some of his earlier work on multiple intelligences. He asserts the criteria he presented in 1983 "does not represent the last word in the identification of intelligences."[1] Moreover he finds psychologists have broadened their definitions of intelligence and increased their tools for measuring intelligence. Recent studies of social intelligence have revealed a set of capacities that are different from standard linguistic and logical intelligences. Although these are the two human intelligences that have historically been valued in school, today a new construct, emotional intelligence, represents a combination of capacities Gardner originally identified as linguistic and logical intelligences.

Rather than restricting emotional intelligence to interpersonal intelligence and intrapersonal intelligence, as he did in his original list, Gardner now sees an emotional intelligence component in each of the intelligences he has named. He writes that he always emphasized his list of intelligences as provisional and continues to believe that they "arise from the combination of a person's genetic heritage and life conditions in a given culture and era."[2] Gardner continues to believe that we each have different kinds of minds because each individual assembles his or her mind in a unique configuration. He acknowledges that what he knew as cognitive science has merged with the study of the brain and what he named as interpersonal intelligence and intrapersonal intelligence is now known as emotional intelligence.

When discussing these issues with author Daniel Goleman, Gardner is quoted as saying, "The time has come to broaden our notion of the spectrum of talents—we've completely lost sight of that. Instead we subject everyone to an education where if you succeed you will be best suited to be a college professor. And we evaluate everyone along the way according to whether they meet that narrow standard of success. We should spend less time ranking children and more time helping them identify their natural competencies and gifts, and cultivate those. There are hundreds and hundreds of ways to succeed, and many, many, different abilities that will help you get there."[3]

Why is Gardner's work relevant when we look at the value of using sign language with your toddler? Gardner is interesting because, although he has never, to our knowledge, spoken or written specifically about sign language, he has always understood the many ways individuals learn and has devoted his life to examining and promoting a variety of ways for children to interface with the world around them. Signing opens a window to a toddler's phase of development that fits well with Gardner's espoused beliefs. Two specific facets of learning he has written about extensively apply to signing. The first of these is symbols and objects, and the second one is flow.

Symbols and Objects

On this topic, Gardner writes an entire chapter, "Knowing the World through Symbols," in his book *The Unschooled Mind: How Children Think and How Schools Should Teach.* He recalls how the life of the blind and deaf writer Helen Keller was dramatically changed when she gained the capacity to name objects. He explains how this ability opens up an entire universe of meaning, not only for Helen Keller, but for any young child. Naming objects allows a toddler to begin to classify and place items in categories. The child progresses and soon can identify both common and differentiating features of objects. Gardner considers naming and classifying to be the central aspects of language acquisition. Once a child acquires this ability, it becomes an indispensable cognitive tool necessary for further language production.

Gardner deems the toddler through preschool years as the symbolic period in a child's life. Throughout the world competence in understanding and using symbols is a universal achievement during this period of children's development. Spoken language is the primary symbol system considered; however, symbols communicated in gestures, pictures, clay, blocks, and toys all add to a toddler's knowledge of the world. A toddler's main job is to gain, as Piaget called it, "symbolic mastery." Achieving this developmental milestone is significant, as it influences all of a child's future learning.

Sign language, because it forms what many have named "word pictures," is useful for capturing the meaning of words. When a toddler is offered this additional visual symbol to augment the sound of a spoken word or the object itself, language acquisition is accelerated. Naming objects and learning language is greatly facilitated when sign language is incorporated into a toddler's life.

Flow

You may ask, what is *flow?* Flow is described as a feeling of joy that is intrinsically rewarding. When you are in flow, you become totally involved in whatever you are doing. Your attention is entirely focused on the task or activity at hand. Time almost seems to stand still. Focus itself appears to lock in, almost making the work or recreation effortless, and you are able to perform at the peak of your capabilities. It is difficult, if not impossible, to be distracted when you are in flow.

Almost everyone has experienced flow at some time. If you reflect on your own past, you will undoubtedly be able to recall times when you have been in flow. A different set of factors will precipitate flow in various individuals. And this is indeed Gardner's point. He encourages educators and parents to provide children with rich environments where they will encounter many opportunities to engage in activities that will allow them to achieve flow.

As a college professor, Marilyn is often in flow when teaching a class. She describes her experiences like this: "Sometimes I am so involved and focused on the interactive process with my students I do not even realize it is time for the period to end. My students tend to be more involved and do not signal me by beginning to pack up their belongings. Sometimes I am actually surprised when students begin to arrive for the class that follows mine."

Ken has expressed the same feeling of flow during his performances. As he engages his audience, a feeling of happiness sweeps over him as his entire attention is focused only on this interaction. There have been times when he was feeling so good that he was captured by flow, losing track of time, and any awareness of interfering background noises.

Howard Gardner sees the positive state of flow as the healthy way for one to teach children. He believes flow motivates a child from within, which he considers to be a practice far superior to external threats or rewards. He states that we should use kids' positive states to "draw them into learning in the domain where they can develop competencies. Flow is an internal state that signifies a kid is engaged in a task that is right. The hope is that when kids gain flow from learning they will be emboldened to take on challenges in new areas."[4]

Marilyn's experience with the young children whom she has encountered as she conducted her sign language research during the past 17 years indicates this is the case. This story of a particular young boy who was a fairly quiet, shy little kindergartner illustrates this phenomenon well.

Signing Success Story

This boy learned to sign and took to it like a duck takes to water. He just loved it, and he was very good at it. The school he attended at the time had engaged the National Theatre of the Deaf to perform for students and parents during an evening assembly to be held in the township's high school auditorium. This five-year-old asked his teachers if he could introduce the National Theatre of the Deaf to the audience using sign language. This child stood alone on a vast stage, proudly signing his introduction to the audience of nearly 1,000 people. He smiled happily as the interpreter voiced his message and then walked confidently off the stage.

The example is typical of what occurs with the vast majority of young children who learn how to communicate with sign language. Initially they are interested in forming words with their hands. They appear to enjoy the physical movement. They are actively watching for the signed response and are eager to continue the signed conversation. And finally, they are not easily distracted.

A Closer Look at Emotional Intelligence

Let's look at emotional intelligence in more detail. The term itself is quite new and has only recently become part of the language. It actually refers to the capacity to acquire and use wisely the following qualities: self-control, zeal, persistence, and the ability to motivate oneself.

Emotional intelligence can be taught to children, but neurological data indicate the existence of a window of opportunity for shaping our children's emotional habits. This opportune period begins in babyhood. However, the prime time for assisting a child to establish healthy emotional reactions is during the toddler years.

When you first begin to consider emotion, it may seem rather complex. Put simply though, emotion is a feeling bursting to express itself through action. The tendency to act is implicit in every strong emotion. Sometimes the action provoked by an emotional feeling is very strong and powerful, resulting in damage to property and people.

Learning to govern the action induced by an emotion is emotional intelligence. Just as children must learn how to hold forks and spoons to feed themselves and learn how to climb into car seats to ride in the car, they must learn how to act when a feeling motivates them. Toddlers who lack the ability to control their emotional outbursts act in the moment of joy or fear or rage. They are unable to reflect and stop the feeling from bursting into action. Such outbursts can soon become habits that undermine good intentions and are clearly destructive.

Medical doctors and researchers are becoming more aware of the role emotions and social interactions play in a child's development. They no longer focus merely on questions about a child's physical development such as walking or skipping. Now physicians are more concerned with a child's emotional, social, and language skills. Dr. Chet Johnson, chairman of the American Academy of Pediatrics' early childhood committee, finds these competencies are considered better predictors of success in adulthood than motor skills. Dr. Stanley Greenspan, clinical professor of psychiatry and pediatrics at George Washington Medical School, is another physician who is actively involved in studying this area. He recently developed a checklist of social and emotional milestones that children should reach by specific ages. He would like doctors to screen their young patients for these milestones.[5]

Dr. Greenspan's preliminary or initial list of milestones commence at 3 months of age. At this first milestone, *opening up*, infants should display deliberate responses and exhibit a calm interest in others, smiling and turning toward them. The second milestone, *diversifying,* occurs at 5 months. By this age, babies should regularly display emotions like surprise, joy, and frustration. Pleasure should be expressed when favorite people are seen. The third milestone is *gazing.* This should happen by the time babies are 10 months old. They should follow their parents' gazes to discover and understand what interests the parents. Babies who have reached the gazing milestone will try to catch the eye of a caregiver and initiate interaction. The fourth and final milestone, *acting out,* is reached at 18 months. As toddlers reach this milestone, they become more self-aware and experience complex emotions such as pride or defiance. These young children should be able to independently solve problems, as well as ask for help when they need it.

Emotional intelligence is central to our human condition. We each have a particular temperament, but the brain circuitry involved is malleable, and during childhood, emotional lessons are learned that shape the emotional intelligence with which individuals will live their lives. Specific physiological reactions to strong emotions prepare the body to respond in a particular manner. With a feeling of anger, blood rushes to the hands to strengthen action. A feeling of fear propels blood to the large skeletal muscles allowing one to flee. With a feeling of happiness, more activity occurs in the brain center that shuts down negative feelings.

Although these physiological reactions occur and come into play, it is crucial for toddlers to become aware of their feelings and learn to respond to them in appropriate ways. The key to sound decision making throughout their lives will depend on how cognizant they are of their feelings and the actions they take in response to them. Toddlers can learn to make appropriate responses to their feelings when parents and caregivers help them shape their behaviors.

The essential foundation for all learning is found in a child's emotional intelligence. The opportunity for shaping this emotional intelligence begins in babyhood and extends throughout childhood. The famed Harvard pediatrician T. Berry Brazelton puts forth the idea that parents can be fine emotional mentors for their infants and toddlers during the crucial preschool period as they help to lay the groundwork for healthy emotional development.[6] Brazelton emphasizes that parents "need to understand how their actions can help generate the confidence, the curiosity, the pleasure in learning and the understanding of limits" in their children that will culminate in their success.[7] The qualities Brazelton names are earmarks of emotional intelligence.

At Durham University in the United Kingdom, Elizabeth Miens devised an investigation in which she studied 200 mothers' abilities to interact with their children and correctly identify their children's emotions. She discovered the toddlers whose "mums" could identify their feelings and guide their children's responses to these feelings progressed the fastest in language and play skills.[8] Meins's research reinforces the findings of others such as Brazelton, Greenspan, Johnson, and of course Goleman, who have shown that helping young children recognize and identify their emotions and training them to act on these feelings in ways that will further their connections to others will significantly increase their communication competency and lead to heightened emotional intelligence.

Self-Control

Self-control is a component of emotional intelligence. An ancillary term that often describes a small piece of this quality is delaying gratification. The capacity to wait or to be patient to the end is the behavior associated with the term. This behavior is very difficult for toddlers. The following classic study demonstrates why helping toddlers achieve the ability to delay gratification bodes well for future success.

At Stanford University the faculty conducted a study in which researchers presented toddlers with a dilemma. The toddlers in the study could have one marshmallow immediately, or they could wait for 15 minutes while the adult ran an errand, and then they could have two marshmallows. The children who succumbed to the temptation, were unable to wait, and ate the single marshmallow represented about one-third of the group. The remaining two-thirds of the group were able to wait the 15 minutes and received the two marshmallows.

The results indicate that the choices the children made had a great deal of bearing on their futures.[9] Nearly 20 years later, the children were tracked down as they graduated from high school. The SAT scores of both groups were examined. The SAT Reasoning Test, formerly named the Scholastic Aptitude Test, is a standardized test for college admissions in the United States. It has two main sections: the mathematics section is widely known as the quantitative section, and the verbal section is often referred to as the critical reading section. The children who had been unable to wait had an average verbal score of 524 and a quantitative score of 528. The children who, as toddlers, had displayed self-control and were able to delay gratification had an average verbal score of

610 and an average quantitative score of 652. Their average total SAT score was 210 points higher than that of the children who had been unable to wait. The disparity between the two groups of children's SAT scores is significant.

This research demonstrates the value of helping your toddler gain self-control and the ability to delay gratification. Put simply, it is teaching your child to wait. You can help your toddler acquire this ability by increasing the enjoyment of waiting. One way to do this is to teach the sign for WAIT. You can reinforce the teaching and the meaning of this word by using the Stop and Wait game you will find in chapter 7.

WAIT—Hold out both open hands, palms up, fingers bent, and wiggle your fingers. Repeat.

You can begin this training in a natural way in response to your toddler's request for a cookie or a ride on a swing. Fairly soon your child will learn that waiting can be fun. The waiting period is fun because your toddler will enjoy the hand movement of the sign WAIT. The reward period is fun as well because your toddler will get a reward after patiently waiting.

Children are not born with the ability to wait. Think back to when your child was a baby and the crying that ensued when the little one's wants and needs were not met swiftly. Assisting a toddler's efforts to gain more self-control and the skills necessary for delaying gratification will make your present life with your toddler more enjoyable. Possessing the ability to wait patiently aids toddlers if they attend nursery school or day care or merely interact with others in the park. In the future, this patient quality taught to toddlers, will help move them to a higher level of academic performance.

Empathy

Empathy is a part of the human equation. It was long thought that babies and young children did not possess empathy, but recent research shows that even young babies will display empathy. Those who are a bit older will try to soothe a crying child or even pull their own mother over to assist a child who is crying in distress. Babies appear to begin learning these behaviors from their parents as they develop into toddlers. Initially they begin by imitating their parents' actions. Also, according to research by Marian Radke-Yarrow and Carolyn Zahn-Waxler, children were more empathetic if parents explained to them how their actions were affecting others. For instance, if one child's words or actions had precipitated distress in another child, then that child's parent would explain that the other child was sad as a result of their behavior.[10]

The difficulty toddlers have managing their complex emotions as they interact with others is widely recognized. Goleman writes that before children can engage others with competence they must first learn some self-control and be able to manage their anger, excitement, impulses, and distress. Empathy, or the ability to know another's feelings, emerges by the age of two. When toddlers respond empathetically, they act in a way that further shapes their feelings. He stresses that "being able to manage emotions in someone else is the core of the art of handling relationships."[11]

It is wise for parents to help their young children acquire and display empathetic reactions to others. We now know that well before children develop oral language they have empathetic feelings and reactions. Without a language to use to communicate their empathetic feelings, they are at a loss. But if they have learned some signs like HAPPY, SAD, and TIRED, they have the ability to communicate their empathetic feelings. (See the glossary for descriptions and pictures of these signs.) This is another instance when using sign language with toddlers offers them an advantage. This type of communication transaction is an additional opportunity for toddlers to recognize, identify, and name their feelings. Such knowledge or ability will also lead to greater emotional intelligence.

Memory

Memory is important for language storage and retrieval. Some of the intricacies relating to memory have been understood for a good number of years while others have been discovered recently and still others continue to puzzle neuroscientists. However, it has been known for some time that languages are stored in the left hemisphere of the brain. Since the work of P. A. Kolers in 1963, the linguistic community has recognized that each language a person knows has its own individual memory store. Kolers's research was repeatedly replicated by others whose outcomes supported his findings. English and Spanish were the two languages used in most of these studies.[12]

When ASL and other signed languages began to be accepted by linguists as true natural languages with all of the properties of an oral or spoken language, a question arose: as a signed language, would ASL have its own memory? To answer this query Harry Hoemann began to conduct research, and in 1978 he published his first findings on the subject, in which he demonstrated that the brain treated a signed language and a spoken language in exactly the same manner. Each language was housed in its own individual memory store.[13]

During the ensuing years Hoemann initiated further studies. In 1990 he and Tonya Koenig, a fellow researcher, published an important study that demonstrated that these individual memory stores for English and ASL were evident after very little knowledge of ASL. This investigation, which was done with beginning students of ASL at Bowling Green State University, showed that after only three weeks of instruction in an ASL class the students established individual memory stores for each language.[14]

If you have considered it important enough to remember the information you have just read in the preceding paragraphs about memory, it is already a memory. Actually, your entire life is a memory, and there are those who would explain that the true reality of your very existence is encoded within language in your memory. The present is a fleeting moment.

Because of this truth, it is crucial to spend some time considering how human beings, particularly toddlers, learn language, store language, and use language to acquire knowledge. As was stated earlier, many facts about language and memory have been known for years, but now it's time to look at some more recent findings. This newer evidence will illustrate how language and memory interact.

A complication of fully understanding memory is that there are various kinds of memory. The brain differentiates between short- and long-term memory. Short-term memory, for example, remembering a phone number long enough to write it down, is controlled by a functional change in the brain. This functional change is described by Eric Kandel as a change in the strength of the communication from one nerve cell to another, a function that is often mediated by a signaling molecule.[15]

Long-term memory, which comes into play when you remember what occurred on your last vacation, involves an anatomical change in the brain. This anatomical change involves the growth and strengthening of synapses, the connections between nerve cells. Within the category of long-term memory are both declarative memories and non-declarative memories. A declarative memory is discreet or explicit, like facts or names. A nondeclarative memory is affected by subliminal messages and often relates to physical activities like riding a bicycle.[16]

The two types of long-term memories described, the declarative and the nondeclarative memories, are intriguing. When children are simultaneously signing and speaking, both of these categories of long-term memory are in play. The spoken word is declarative. The physical sign is nondeclarative. In a like manner, when children are looking at their parents and simultaneously seeing and hearing words, they are experiencing both declarative and non-declarative memories at the same time.

Short-term memory is converted to long-term memory by repetition. In other words—practice. Memory storage depends on strengthening the connections, or synapses, between brain cells. Every synaptic exchange fosters an association. You might be aware of this association between or among memories if you've ever had difficulty recalling an actor's name. You may have a mental picture of the actor and know the names of several of his movies and perhaps even the latest gossip concerning him; notwithstanding all of this information, you cannot remember his name.

What are the implications of these facts about memory on the use of sign language with your toddler? There are several.

The physical structure of the human brain actually changes through the process of learning. This aspect suggests that your efforts to teach your child to sign will have a potential lasting effect on your child's future.

Also, because of these facts, your child will be able to access the left hemisphere of the brain and find two separate places, two memory stores, to search when trying to locate a word. The word may either be in the English language memory store or in the ASL (sign) memory store. In either case, due to the fact that there is a built-in language redundancy in the brain, a toddler will literally have double the chance of coming up with the word that is being sought. The redundancy translates to an increased ability to communicate. Generally, this increased ability to communicate offers a toddler higher self-esteem, a larger English vocabulary, and a greater comfort level in communicating. All of these attributes are qualities that lead to healthy emotional intelligence.

The Structure and Function of the Brain

In Daniel Goleman's preface to Sharon Begley's *Train Your Mind, Change Your Brain,* he emphasizes that an investigation focusing on neuroplasticity, or the brain's capacity to change, would not have been possible a decade ago. The new findings researchers are discovering are important because, for over a century, neuroscience experts held the belief that the brain takes its shape during the childhood years and does not possess the capability to change its structure later in life. Current research has now replaced that long-held belief, and neuroscience is now exploring the many ways the brain continues to reshape itself throughout life.[17]

The understanding of how a child's brain is structured and how it functions has radically changed since the 19th century when William James said infants are born into "one great blooming, buzzing confusion."[18] Today it is recognized that the brain of a newborn baby is not fully developed; indeed if it were, the infant would not be able to fit through the birth canal. The brain matures in the world, primarily during the first three years of life.

The immature brain of a child is remarkably malleable. The basis for the plasticity of the developing brain is its extreme redundancy. A one-year-old has twice as many neuronal connections as an adult. Each of the 100 billion neurons in the newborn brain connects to an average of 2,500 other neurons. For the next three years most of the other neurons continue to connect until they form an average of 15,000 synapses. That is as connected as the brain will ever become (figure 1).

After the age of three, the process of pruning begins and the child loses, on average, about half of the connections. The neurons that once met through a synapse no longer have the capacity to meet because the synapse, or road, that connected them has disappeared. The synapses that remain are the ones that are most traveled. The side-street or back-road synapses gradually deteriorate and are lost.[19]

Particularly during early childhood, the synaptic connections are sculpted by sensory experience. Helping your child establish and maintain more synapses may be akin to having a savings account. Even after pruning, additional synapses remain and can be called upon should the need arise.

When the ABC evening anchor Bob Woodruff was badly wounded in Iraq, he suffered serious brain injuries. His wife, Lee, recounts that the doctors assured her Bob had a greater chance of recovery because he had developed more synapses in his brain. His physician, Dr. Armonda, explained: "If you

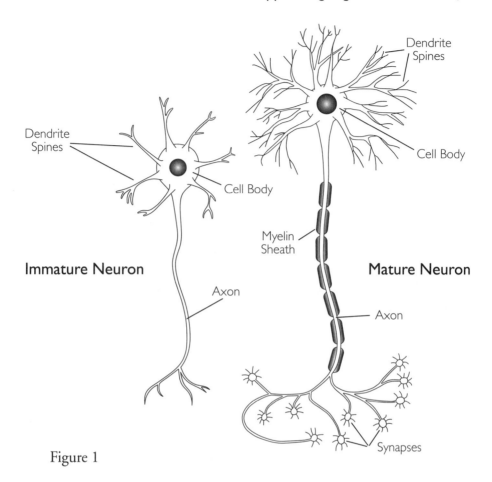

Figure 1

are a person who sharpens pencils for a living and have a brain injury, you will probably not have as many neurons from your former life to help rehabilitate yourself. But if you are a person…who has made great use of your brain, speaks multiple languages, has intellectual curiosity, and abundant life experiences, you have a better chance at how those neurons are going to reconnect—you have more chance to develop alternate pathways for cognitive function and reasoning and putting all those neurons back together again."[20]

This may appear to be a far-reaching example to use in a book with a focus on toddlers, but as we all know, we have no certain knowledge of the future. As parents, we want to prepare our children for their tomorrows. Providing the optimum number of opportunities for toddlers to establish synapses in their brain increases the likelihood their achievements will be greater. In the event a brain injury should befall them, they, like Bob Woodruff, would have a greater chance of recovery.

David Linden stresses that the brain is massively interconnected and indicates there is a good reason for these multiple connections to be initiated. The multiple attempts to form synapses are necessary because when the connections between neurons are formed, only 30 percent of the signals actually establish a workable link. The significant uncertainty of the formation of synapses indicates the need for as much repetition as possible when teaching or training your toddler. Offering a word in both spoken English and an ASL manual sign will increase the likelihood that your child will comprehend the word as well as retain the word.[21]

The brain, as you undoubtedly learned in school, is organized in a specific manner with various sections relegated to perform particular functions (figure 2). The visual cortex processes signals from the eye, the motor cortex processes a person's movements, for example, when you move your hand, and the somatosensory cortex processes the sense of touch, though it does not register expected sensations such as the feeling of clothing. To early researchers this meant the cluster of neurons in the visual cortex will only process signals from the eye, and the cluster of neurons in the motor cortex will only cause people to make intentional movements. This ostensibly remains true. However, it is now known that all the neurons remain the same, and it does not matter in which cortex they are found. The brain's structures are not stuck with their intended function. One cortex can take over for another cortex. This cross-modality plasticity accounts for the superior tactile and perceptual abilities of blind children. Brain specialization is not derived from anatomy; it is the result of experience. You might say that the brain's environment, culture, and community all determine the functional properties of its neurons.[22]

A fine example of the interconnectedness of the various aspects of the brain and the body is the use of the hands. Toddlers love to touch objects, manipulate switches, and roll little toy cars. The information they gather in this manner is written into the tactile kinesthetic of manipulation and movement. It is returned to the brain and compared with the information from the visual system as part of the process through which the brain creates visuospatial images. Through this exchange between the brain and the hand, a kind of dual learning takes place. As the late Canadian author Robertson Davies wrote, "The hand speaks to the brain as surely as the brain speaks to the hand."[23]

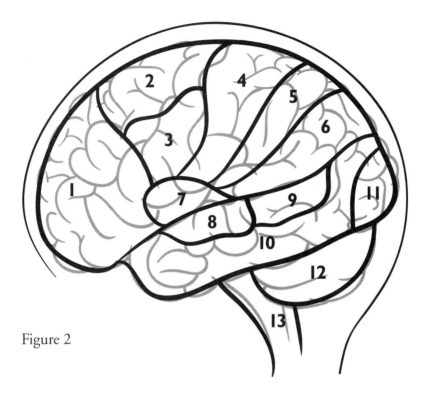

Figure 2

Complex abilities result from the cooridination of many brain areas!

1. **Prefrontal cortex**—involved in thinking, planning, and short-term memory
2. **Supplementary Motor Cortex**—organizes sequence of movement
3. **Premotor Cortex**—selects the movement
4. **Primary Motor Cortex**—gives order to carry out movement
5. **Primary Somatosensory Cortex**—processes the sense of touch
6. **Posterior Parietal Cortex**—integration of visual and motor signals
7. **Broca's Area**—grammar processing
8. **Auditory Cortex**—identifies sounds and their locations
9. **Wernicke's Area**—controls language, meaning of words
10. **Hippocampus**—memory and learning area
11. **Visual Cortex**—processes signals from eyes
12. **Cerebellum**—balance and coordinates movement
13. **Brain Stem**—controls breathing, heart rate, etc.

Frank Wilson, a neurologist from the University of California School of Medicine in San Francisco who authored *The Hand: How Its Use Shapes the Brain, Language and Human Culture,* would surely agree with Davies' quote. Wilson credits the work of the 19th century Scottish surgeon and anatomy teacher Sir Charles Bell as his inspiration. Bell's insight into the interconnectedness among movement, perception, and learning was revolutionary for his time. He stressed the interdependence of hand and brain function. According to Bell, both the hand and the eye develop as sense organs through practice, as the brain teaches itself by making the hand and eye learn to work together. The brain constructs messages based on the images received from the eye and the hand. It records a collection of sensory data derived from eye and limb movements. Bell's assertions about the coupling of hand and eye movement and the relationship of this process to the emergence of thought and language development are borne out by Wilson's findings.[24]

Wilson emphasizes the point that the thought-language connection becomes a hand-thought-language nexus. The child learns with real objects, unified through a sequence of actions organizing a child's active movements and sensorimotor explorations. Wilson goes on to stress that "none of the neurophysiological brain activity can be related to real language until it gains access to an input-output channel."[25]

Sign language is eminently suited to serve as the input-output channel. When connections between language and thought are formed with sign language, language and thought are intrinsically attached to what is happening to the child's hand. As the brain learns to send and receive signed messages, language milestones occur in concert with motor milestones, developing on parallel tracks but always interconnected, interdependent, growing, reinforcing, and influencing each other. Sign language has a unique capacity to tap into the natural exchange between hand and brain, optimizing the emergence of language in the child because of the physiological advantage ASL has over English.

In *The New Brain,* the neurologist and neuropsychiatrist Richard Restak describes what is happening in the brain when the hand moves. An MRI shows three distinct parts of the brain are activated. The prefrontal cortex is responsible for the intention to move, the supplementary motor cortex organizes the sequence for the move, and the primary motor cortex gives the order to carry out the move.[26]

Restak reports about a study conducted at the National Institutes of Health (NIH) in which a sequence of finger movements, similar to ASL signs or the manual alphabet, was taught. From the first day of instruction, new neurons were observed in the three brain cortexes involved in the movement sequence. More neurons were evident after each practice session. As the formation of motor skills increased, so did the neurons. A year later, with no more training, the brain changes remained, and the study participants could repeat the motor skills.

Experimental findings from a mirroring-process study amplify the previous material concerning the NIH's movement-sequence and brain-change research. In this related investigation, subjects were monitored with brain scans while they watched movements they would later imitate. While the participants observed the movements, the brain was activated in the same regions that would be involved in actually performing the actions. This indicates that during the observation period, the three brain areas responsible for generating the hand movements were, in essence, practicing.[27]

Parents are engaged in the mirroring process when they show their children how to form a sign. It is intriguing to realize that before children even attempt to form the signs, their brains have been activated in the areas necessary for carrying out the movements of the sign. When they actually learn to imitate the movements and form the sign, additional neurons are engaged and new synapses are established in their brains. So, first children learn from observing the sign and then they learn from making the sign.

Neuroscience provides further insight into what is happening in a child's brain as it continues to mature. A general principal of reinforcement through repetition persists. As the connections between neurons are formed, the synapses involved are strengthened by repetition. An apt analogy to explain the power of repetition is this: If you make a path through a field but only occasionally use the path, it will soon disappear, and you will no longer be able to find the path. But if you use the path several times a day, it will be easy to locate. Repetitive exercises activate relevant brain circuits or synapses and sharpen their connections. This basic principle holds true for anything anyone wants to learn at any age. It is impossible to overstate the impact of repetition on the maturing brain of a young child. Toddlers have the most to gain from reinforcement through repetition.

Richard Restak examines what some call tacit knowledge and others call implicit knowledge. Both of these terms refer to the human brain's ability to act automatically after a physical activity becomes routine. When toddlers sign, they are using implicit knowledge. Neuroscientists refer to this thinking without conscious effort as the "cognitive unconscious."[28] As the parent teaching your child to sign, you may begin to unconsciously sign when you are attempting to communicate. This begins to happen when you are engaged with your child or other family members, but before long you may be adding signs to your spoken words when you are out in the world. It often happens to Marilyn, and in fact, this is why Georgia and Ken began and continued to sign with their children.

To sum up, signing can become a routine physical activity. When this occurs, the brain is acting automatically. In the vernacular, it is called muscle memory. In the parlance of neuroscience, it is the cognitive unconscious, or implicit or tacit knowledge. No matter what you call it, having it is crucial. It affords a toddler what we call a "Jump Start on Smart."

Delayed Speech

Many parents believe that signing with their toddler will delay speech development. This is incorrect. The opposite is true. Signing with toddlers increases both their ability and their desire to speak.

Toddlers want to communicate. However, young children are often unable to use spoken language. For such children it must be like being trapped in a foreign land where no one understands a word they say. It has to be frustrating. The absence of an ability to communicate leads to anger, crying, and emotional outbursts—all of the behaviors associated with the label "terrible twos."

Delayed speech can occur for several reasons. The physical ability to speak occurs typically in children when they are between 12 and 18 months of age. It is different for each child. In the same way that all children do not walk at the same age, they do not all begin to talk at the same age. Also, when they begin to walk, some stay upright and never crawl again, and some continue to do both for a fairly long time. Speech develops similarly. The age when a child begins to use words varies. A child's ability to pronounce words clearly and accurately differs from child to child. Vocabulary size, sentence structure, and enthusiasm and comfort with communicating are all additional variables. The constant is that every child has a great physiological need to communicate and a great desire to communicate.

Well before children have the ability to produce spoken language they have begun to respond to spoken English. They already comprehend some words. By adding signs to the words that toddlers understand such as milk, tired, cookie, cat, or dog, preverbal toddlers have a way to communicate with their parents.

This is a great benefit for parents because they can figure out what the child wants. Burton White, an educational psychologist and the author of *The First Three Years of Life,* notes that the second year of life is a time when most children, and especially boys, have very little spoken language. White believes toddlers with an absence of a means to communicate can cause a good deal of grief for their parents, as the parents have trouble understanding their children's needs and desires.[29]

Some children experience further delay in gaining the ability to speak for any number of reasons. Sometimes it is a single cause, and other times multiple causes are at work. They can be physiological or psychological. Some may be associated with disease or illness. Often parents, physicians, or educators are unsure of the reason for the speech delay.

When a child has delayed speech, the recommended solution is generally to teach the child to sign. Historically, the earliest use of sign language with hearing children was with children who had delayed speech. It is crucial that children have the ability to use language. Sign language offers them the means to communicate. The use of language and communication is necessary for toddlers' emotional health, as well as their mental growth and development.

Toddlers who experience language delays are using sign language in many schools. Teachers in such schools see signing as a means to speech. They believe it is an effective tool that offers visual cues for their students. With sign language, it is easier for children with language delays to follow directions, and signing can also help them make connections between words and concepts and ultimately lead them to speak.

"Sign language is often used by speech therapists as a first step when they are working with children who are not talking or who have limited language," according to Lisa Wright a speech pathologist with Virginia Commonwealth University's Virginia Treatment Center for Children. "They're not using words for whatever reason—it might be a motor thing or a cognitive thing—but using hands is a bridge to learning words," Wright said. She uses sign language most with preschoolers and toddlers. Many of the children have problems that go beyond simple language delay. The first signs she teaches are easy words like MORE or JUICE. Next come BALL and BOOK. Knowing just a few signs enables the toddlers to communicate on a basic level that can reduce their frustration and often eliminate negative behaviors.

Wright continued: "They have this need and nobody understands what they want. So if you give them the tools, they don't need to act out anymore."

After establishing some basic communication, the next step for Wright and others is to help the children learn to speak. Wright goes on to explain that signing is a critical part of the process. "For some of these little guys, I wouldn't say they would never talk, but I think not learning sign would delay the process. I think they would plateau and just get stuck. It would take longer."[30]

MORE—Hold the thumb and fingertips of both hands together (as you do with one hand for EAT) and then tap them together. Repeat.

JUICE—Sign the letter J by your cheek. Then add the sign for DRINK by shaping your hand like a cup and tipping it towards your mouth.

BALL—With fingers spread and curved, tap the fingertips of both hands together at chest level. Repeat.

BOOK—Hold your flat hands together at chest level. Open your hands while keeping the little fingers touching (as if you are opening a book).

The Science behind Signed Responses

It is important to understand the salient reasons for using a signed response with your toddler. To amplify this idea, let's examine the physiological difference between a verbal response and a signed response. The research indicates a signed response offers clear beneficial effects in several realms.

You use words to shape your child's behavior. You have done this since your child was born. Of course, at the beginning, a child does not fully comprehend the meaning of your words. Their understanding is aided by the cues they receive from your tone of voice, from your facial expression, and from your rate of delivery. These pieces of what linguists call paralanguage all contribute to a young child's ability to grasp meaning from spoken words.

When you begin to include signs with your spoken words, you are enhancing the quality of your communication. In addition to the spoken words coupled with the typical paralanguage, your child is receiving an entirely new set of signals. Watching your hands as you form the signs presents new data from which the toddler gathers information.

As a toddler starts to learn the signs and is able to form them, you can begin to encourage your child to make a signed response when you ask the child a question or want them to comply with a request. The signs should accompany a spoken response if the child is able to pronounce the words. For instance, if you say and sign: "PLEASE FIND your SHOES," your child would respond by signing and saying "SHOES" or "FIND SHOES" or, for some, maybe even "I FIND SHOES."

PLEASE—Rub a flat hand, palm in, in a circular motion on your chest.

FIND—Hold your left hand flat, palm up. Make the number 5 with your right hand, palm down and above your left hand, extend your index finger and thumb onto the palm of your left hand, pinch them together, and move your right hand upward a short distance, forming the letter F.

SHOE—Make the letter S with both hands, palms down and apart. Tap the sides of your fists together twice.

I / ME—Hold your fist up with your index finger out, and point to the middle of your chest.

When toddlers make signed responses they will acquire two separate memories of the communication. They will have both a voiced-aural memory and a visual-kinesthetic memory of the encounter. Each of these memories will be stored in a separate memory store in your child's brain. Both of the memories will be available for your child. This establishes a healthy redundancy. In a sense, it is similar to placing the message in two computer programs such as Word and WordPerfect.

At a minimum, double the number of new synapses will be formed as both versions of the message are encoded in a toddler's memory. This signed response increases the likelihood toddlers will recall your directions and act on them appropriately. As previously indicated, using the signed response is also very helpful when encouraging toddlers to recognize their feelings and act on them in a proper manner.

Conclusion

Many aspects of the benefits of using sign language with toddlers have been covered in this chapter. They include but are not limited to multiple intelligences, symbols and objects, flow, self-control and empathy, memory, delayed speech, and structure and function of the brain. Every one of these areas is important and the benefits derived from signing with toddlers are inherent in each of them.

Notwithstanding these benefits, the present and future life of toddlers will be immeasurably enhanced by using signs to help them recognize, identify, and understand their feelings. You can provide them with ample opportunities to respond to these feelings with good behavioral choices. Encourage toddlers to practice their responses to their feelings with signs. Give them many opportunities to give you a signed response. As Brazelton, Goleman, and Gardner know, emotional intelligence is learned. Incorporating sign language into the training you offer your child will foster more success than you might imagine. We believe it is impossible to overstate the case for the value of using sign language with your toddler.

Chapter 3
Why Use ASL?

American Sign Language is the unvoiced language used by members of the Deaf community. It is a popular and modern language that is commonly used in the United States. In addition to fulfilling foreign or modern language requirements in high schools and colleges, ASL is being used to encourage early communication in hearing babies, as well as to promote literacy in early childhood education.

All of these facts were not always true about ASL. This chapter will cover why ASL is a popular language today and relate some of its history. It will clarify the reasons why all Sign to Speak materials recommend ASL signs rather than signs that you might make up yourself.

The Origins of Sign Language

During the early 19th century, the United States was experiencing a surge in philanthropy, providing individuals who were considered unfortunate with needed support. A group of Connecticut benefactors led by Mason Cogswell, who himself had a daughter who was deaf, were interested in providing education for the young deaf population of New England which, based on evidence gathered at the time, included about 400 prospective students. Thomas Hopkins Gallaudet, Cogswell's neighbor and a young Yale graduate, was sent to Europe to observe and learn the methods used for teaching in European schools for the Deaf. Gallaudet's goal was to bring this education to the United States.

French Sign Language

After first unsuccessfully exploring what the United Kingdom had to offer, Gallaudet was welcomed at the French School for the Deaf. He was captivated by two young Deaf teachers at the Paris school, Jean Massieu and Laurent Clerc. Gallaudet watched them teach and took classes from them. He was impressed with the breadth of their knowledge and depth of their understanding. Massieu's description of the meaning of the word *gratitude* as "memory of the heart" charmed him. Gallaudet proposed that Clerc come to the United States and serve as a teacher in the school he intended to establish. After gaining permission from Abbe Sicard, the principal of the school, and sadly bidding his mother good-bye, Clerc joined Gallaudet on his journey across the ocean.

During the voyage, Gallaudet taught Clerc English, and Clerc taught Gallaudet sign language and the manual alphabet. This alphabet, a one-handed way to signify every letter in the written alphabet, is an integral part of the language and is used to spell words. The sign language that Clerc taught Gallaudet was French Sign Language (LSF). This was the indigenous sign language of deaf French natives coupled with methodical markers introduced by the Abbe de l'Epee. As a parish priest, de l'Epee had encountered children in the Deaf community using signs. He learned their language and used it to teach them to read and write French. In 1755 de l'Epee founded the world's first public school for children who were deaf.

The American School for the Deaf

Clerc and Gallaudet landed in the United States on August 9, 1816, and opened their school on August 15, 1817, with Gallaudet as the principal and Clerc as the head teacher. It was the first school for the Deaf in the nation. As it grew, this school would move to three locations in the Hartford, Connecticut, area. Today, it is called the American School for the Deaf and is known as the mother school of 64 similar schools in this country.

A large number of the early students at the school came from Martha's Vineyard. Others, who came from a variety of places in New England, arrived using what were commonly known as home signs. Home signs are signs that originated within the homes of Deaf individuals. They are generally created by the Deaf person and shared with family members. This is the genesis of all sign systems and is similar to the difference between a dialect and standard American English in spoken language. These various forms of signing gradually melded with the French Sign Language used by Clerc and Gallaudet into a unified manner of signing that would eventually be known as American Sign Language.

Clerc and Gallaudet each fell in love with and married Deaf students from the school. Both of these young women would outlive their husbands and become significant contributors to the Deaf community and the continued use of sign language within it.

Sophia Fowler, Gallaudet's wife, became the mother of eight children, all of whom were native signers. In 1857, her youngest son, Edward Miner Gallaudet, founded the institution now known as Gallaudet University in Washington DC. She joined Edward in Washington and served as matron of the fledgling school. At the time she was in her 60s, her 20-year-old son wrote that he believed she gave an air of dignity and distinction to the establishment. His mother was always the model for him of what a Deaf person could accomplish. He found the sign language they had always used for communication to be a rich and rewarding language that was every bit as capable of encoding abstract ideas as English.

Sign language was always the language used for instruction at the American School, and it continued as the language for instruction at the Washington institution under the direction of Edward Miner Gallaudet. The majority of teachers in both schools were Deaf, and the students flourished academically during this early period with its strong sign language focus. Their Deaf instructors used sign language to teach their courses and taught English only as a written language. There was never confusion between language and speech because speech was not equated with language. The students could read, write, and understand English and also use sign language to communicate. They knew two languages, English and sign language.

The Language of ASL

William Stokoe, an English professor at Galludet University, was familiar with the sign language the students were using on campus, and he studied this signing in his laboratory tucked away in the university basement. He published his groundbreaking book *Sign Language Structure* in 1960, demonstrating that sign language was indeed a complete independent language with all the hallmarks of any language. The initial reaction to his endeavors was lukewarm. However, his ideas were gradually accepted and adopted.

Stokoe has become world famous for his research and is recognized as the primary person responsible for identifying the true nature of American Sign Language. Because he realized that the intricate movements of his students' hands and bodies represented a fully developed language that met all linguistic criteria, he is often identified as the Father of American Sign Language. Surprisingly, Dr. Stokoe did not see the full language legitimacy he and those who followed him bestowed on ASL as his greatest accomplishment. Rather, he explains, "What I consider my principal discovery is how language must have begun as Sign. That is to say briefly: an upright walking visually oriented, late evolving primary species began to see that body movements really did mean what they looked as if they meant. Voice can make sound but the only way that a wealth of meanings can be connected to sounds is by being told what the sounds mean. If gestures had developed into actual language—and much sign research shows they have done so—then sounds habitually uttered along with gestures would have become connected with meanings that the gestures had naturally signified."[1]

Ultimately, other linguists supported Stokoe's view and recognized ASL as a true language. With this understanding of it as an actual complete, albeit unvoiced, language, ASL began to receive acceptance in a wider venue. It was used to fulfill modern or foreign language requirements, first in colleges and universities and soon in high schools. Since 1987, ASL has fulfilled foreign language requirements in California high schools. It is now accepted as a modern language in virtually all of the states and is taught as such in many secondary schools.

ASL as a Teaching Tool

Beginning in the 1980s, signing found its way into mainstream education for typical hearing students. Preschool, kindergarten, and elementary teachers discovered ASL. The manual alphabet helped their students recognize letters and words, helped with phonemic awareness, and benefited their literacy development.

In this book we use the same manual alphabet and signs for concepts and words as the Deaf community, but we do not use the syntax or word order of ASL. Instead, we use what is called Contact Signing, the combination of ASL signs and concepts with spoken-English word order, since your primary purpose for using ASL is to facilitate your toddler's comprehension and use of the English language.

ASL word order is quite different from English word order. In general, ASL word order is the reverse of English, where we place the descriptor before the object, as in a white house, or a large brown leather chair and so on. In ASL the order would be house white and chair leather brown large. ASL also uses a particular order to describe others. The gender is always first, followed by height, body type, color of hair, and hairstyle.

The Advantages of ASL

Gallaudet found that sign language had many advantages. He thought the meanings of words were more easily understood in sign and that forming the manual alphabet would aid in remembering words and their spellings. He believed it was good for hearing siblings of the students of the American School to learn sign language, not only to enable them to communicate with their sisters and brothers but for their own benefit. Gallaudet was certain that the more varied the forms of language, whether voiced or manual, the better it would be understood and recalled by children.

Nearly 200 years after Gallaudet set forth his beliefs about the multiple benefits of sign language, current research and our newest technologies are providing support for his insights. Marilyn's research demonstrates the enhanced spelling ability of students who use the manual alphabet as a spelling aid. More than a dozen of her published works show that when you use sign language with children, they will have a 20 percent larger receptive English vocabulary.

Why Not Use Made-Up Signs and Gestures?

There are five great reasons for using American Sign Language instead of made-up signs and gestures.

1. ASL is a structured language with vocabulary that exists and dictionaries you can access for existing signs.
2. It is one of the most common languages in the United States so by teaching ASL vocabulary you are giving your toddler the foundations for learning a "real" second language.
3. American Sign Language is recognized and used by millions of people across the United States. It is becoming ever more popular as its use increases each year with children from cradle to college.
4. It is taught in preschools and schools across the country. When children encounter it, they will already have knowledge of and vocabulary for ASL that is in common with other children.
5. It will allow your child to interact with Deaf children and the Deaf community when encountered.

Conclusion

Parents and caregivers are offered a variety of choices for signing with their children. Our view is that American Sign Language vocabulary is the preferred method in regard to the use of signs with toddlers. ASL is a major language in the United States having grown and developed its own structure, alphabet, and vocabulary, and it is well established. By using ASL, you are introducing a second language that exists right alongside spoken English. It is universal and is used and recognized by millions of people.

ASL keeps your endeavor simple. It standardizes the words you will be using and provides you with dictionaries and other ways to develop signs that are of interest to you and your toddler. And, unlike home or personal signs, if you forget a word, you can just look it up. Finally, as toddlers grow into other childhood stages, ASL can grow easily with them providing the same benefits for communication and language development right into elementary school.

PART 2

How to Sign with Toddlers

Chapter 4
Get a Jump Start on Smart

Signing with toddlers offers many more options for parents, teachers, and caregivers than signing with babies. Some of the same concepts used with babies continue to work, but the reasons for and the range of signing activities for toddlers is very different. If you have been signing with your baby, continue with the signs and methods that you have found effective. If you are just starting to sign with a toddler, you are beginning at a very exciting time. Toddlers have longer attention spans and more muscle control than babies, and their curiosity and interests are expanding rapidly. Signing is extremely beneficial as it provides them with greater language skills and as much as twice the usable vocabulary of nonsigning children. The result is enhanced communication and the fostering of enthusiasm for learning that can last a lifetime.

Parents of toddlers are faced with children that are highly mobile, full of energy and are exploring their world with enthusiasm. They are demanding, lovable, absorbing information rapidly, building language, and into almost everything. Toddlers are capable of using and understanding lots of words.

In our first book, *Babies Can Talk,* we focused our attention on providing signs that would allow babies to express their wants and needs. Effective signs like EAT, MORE, and ALL DONE (which are found in the glossary of this book) were suggested, and though they are still effective, signing with toddlers takes on new dimensions. In this book *Toddlers at Play,* we are offering your toddler signs that are effective in

- shaping behavior
- fostering self-control
- supporting the learning of feelings and empathy
- enhancing communication
- enriching language growth
- developing an enthusiasm for learning

Start Signing Right Now

This chapter offers you six highly effective signs that have been used successfully with toddlers. These signs will help you with silent behavior control, encourage empathy, enhance communication and reward your toddler's efforts. You will find over 200 possible signs to use with your toddler included in this book. However, we believe the Jump Start on Smart signs of STOP, GENTLE, HELP, CHANGE, HURT, and GOOD are the best to begin with. Incorporate these signs into your daily life and you will soon see just how wonderful signing will be for you and your toddler.

Keep It Simple Signing Rules

Here are a few "Keep It Simple Rules" to help you be successful at signing with your toddler:

1. Focus on a few signs at a time and slowly introduce new ones.
2. Have your toddler's attention and be sure you are looking at each other.
3. Sign correct signs even if your child develops an alternative version.

4. Clearly enunciate each word you sign.
5. Repeat signs often and throughout the day.
6. Create signing opportunities that will help you reinforce the signs you are using.
7. Include signing in your playtime activities. Sign while reading, storytelling, playing games, and singing songs.
8. Keep signing fun and playful. Never be coercive.

STOP

The sign for the word STOP is one of the most used signs for parents and caregivers of toddlers. Toddlers love getting into everything, and this sign will provide you with an effective way to control and shape behavior. STOP will remain effective with a child for years to come. It requires an action and response from your toddler without you having to raise your voice. Use facial expressions to demonstrate how serious you are in your request to STOP something.

Signing Success Story

When Ken and Georgia's son John was about 2½ years old, they enrolled him in a swimming class. During the class John kept running along the side of the pool to get from one place to another. He was just an excited young boy, but he needed to learn to walk and not run on a wet pool deck. The other parents, whose children were also running, were constantly screaming to their children, "Walk!" or "Stop running!"

Ken, who was sitting on the side of the pool opposite to John, noticed that John would look at him just before he began to run. So Ken began to sign STOP and WALK every time John looked from across the pool. John would smile and walk to *where he was going. Never once did Ken raise his voice like the other parents.*

One of the moms commented to Ken a few weeks later, "You're really a nice dad. You never yell!" Another mom then added, "You're so lucky to have such a well-behaved child." What these parents did not realize was that Ken was actively communicating, shaping, and controlling John's behavior during the class. He was not screaming; rather he was effectively interacting with John by using sign language.

STOP is a useful sign for stopping an unwanted behavior, and as you saw from the story, it can be done silently. You could sign to your toddler to STOP climbing on something, or stop throwing food on the floor, or stop pulling the dog's tail, and so on.

STOP—Hold your left hand, palm up and extended. Hold your right flat hand facing in and chop it down quickly, laying it on top of your left hand. Use your facial expression to reinforce how strongly you mean STOP.

GENTLE

Chapter 1 explained the importance of developing empathy. Toddlers can get carried away and get a bit rough with others, including family pets. Parents are always looking for ways to help their children see that they need to control their own behavior and that they need to be kind and considerate of others. The key word and sign for parents to use to help develop empathy is GENTLE.

GENTLE is effective when you sign it and then demonstrate what it means. You can demonstrate GENTLE by softly touching a child or softly petting an animal as you say the word and then by following up that action with signing and saying the word. In this case, you are connecting the sign to the spoken word and to the meaning of the word through an activity.

GENTLE—Hold one hand flat, palm down. Then gently stroke the back of that hand.

Signing Success Story

Sarah had two boys who were just a little over one year apart in age, and her oldest was having difficulty being gentle with his brother. Sarah worked repeatedly for a few weeks signing GENTLE, saying the word, and physically demonstrating what it meant. When Richie was being too rough with his younger brother, Matthew, she would say and sign "GENTLE Richie, be GENTLE." After a few weeks of this, the result was that Richie would almost always stop being rough and look at Sarah signing and saying GENTLE. She knows this sign has helped her reduce the roughhousing that almost always ends with one of the boys getting hurt.

HELP

Meaningful interactions and connected moments with children do not need to be accidents. You can arrange for these special times to happen. You can empower your toddlers to be involved with you beyond playtimes or activity times by involving them in signing throughout the day. One of the better toddler words for achieving this is the word HELP.

Signing Success Story

Georgia started working at the School for the Deaf at 6:00 a.m. On her first day, the other counselor took Georgia to the dorm and explained that her job was to wake up the boys, help them get dressed and ready for breakfast, and then get them off to school. Georgia knew no signs. She had taught herself finger spelling, thinking that this would come in handy, not considering that 5- and 6-year-olds don't know how to spell well. The counselor showed her the sign for WAKE UP, and then Georgia was supposed to work on her own. The first little boy jumped out of bed and started signing. Fortunately, the other counselor was still there and told her that Kevin needed HELP with his shirt. Georgia woke up the next boy, who needed HELP making his bed. Later, she was asked to HELP with tying shoes, buckling belt buckles, combing hair, opening toothpaste tubes, buttoning shirts, sprinkling salt on eggs, and buttering toast. After two hours she knew over 30 words, but the one that was used most often and got her attention the fastest was when the children needed HELP.

HELP is a wonderful word to encourage your child to be involved in daily activities. For example, you can say "HELP Mommy put the toys away" or "HELP me put the clothes away" or HELP with other activities around the house. It is good to learn a few signs for things that your toddler may be helping with around the house like TOYS (BALL and TRAIN) or CLOTHES (SHOES and SOCKS). All of these words and more can be found in the glossary.

HELP—Hold one hand in a fist, thumb up, and the other hand flat, palm up. Lay your fist on top of your palm. Then lift both hands as if one hand is helping the other. Use your fist hand in the event that you cannot do a two-handed sign.

CHANGE

Toddlers will soon be transitioning from diapers to being toilet trained. While they are still in diapers, a wonderful word that enhances communication by allowing them to express a specific need is the word CHANGE. We have suggested for years that the word CHANGE be used instead of diaper as it is an easy sign for toddlers to do, and once they are out of diapers, they can continue to use it. For example, your toddler can ask to CHANGE her shirt or CHANGE her toy or even to CHANGE the DVD that you put on for her to watch.

CHANGE—Make the letter X with both hands, one on top of the other, with your palms facing each other. Twist your hands so that they switch position. The opposite hand is now on top.

HURT

Toddlers are very active. They are constantly running, walking, and falling. HURT is a useful sign to help your toddler, sometimes through his tears, to tell you what is wrong. This sign is a directional sign that is signed where you are hurting. For example, if you had a headache, you would sign it near your head. If you hurt your knee, you would sign it near your knee and so on. You can also teach this sign effectively by demonstrating the sign for HURT on yourself when you bump your leg, hurt your arm, or stub a toe.

HURT—With both hands in fists, point index fingers toward each other and tap the fingertips together. Remember that this sign is directional. Sign it near the place where you hurt.

GOOD

Toddlers respond well to parental praise. It seems to be in their nature to want to please others and strive to do more and learn more to receive acclaim. The sign for GOOD provides you with a word that rewards actions in a positive and physically expressive way. It is also visually engaging since signing GOOD requires you and your toddler to be looking at each other.

GOOD—Hold your right hand flat, near your mouth, then move it down to your left hand, which is held with the palm up in front of you. Both palms will be facing up, with the back of your right hand on the palm of your left hand.

Conclusion

You can get started signing right away with just a few signs. In this chapter we focused on six very effective signs to use with a toddler: STOP, GENTLE, HELP, CHANGE, HURT, and GOOD. These signs will assist you in shaping a toddler's behavior in positive ways. These words help them to be actively involved in daily activities and in praising and rewarding their efforts. To establish these signs, just as with other signs in the future, you will need to incorporate them into your life, sign them every time you say them, and invent ways to create signing situations. For example, you can sign "HELP Mommy around the house," "It's time to STOP what we are doing," or "Let's GENTLY put away all the toys." Whenever you choose to reinforce your communication by signing with your toddler, be sure that you sign with a playful and attentive attitude.

Chapter 5
Master the Basics

Signing with toddlers is a fun and playful activity that provides them with a way to learn, remember, and use lots of vocabulary. It is not difficult to do; parents can easily learn how to use sign language and this chapter offers the basic information to be successful. If you master the basics, signing can develop into a rewarding family adventure.

Your Toddler's Development

As discussed previously in this book, children develop in a variety of ways, so here are some additional thoughts that will help you to understand why signing is so effective. In our first book, *Babies Can Talk,* we talked about Erik Erikson and his first stage of development called Trust versus Mistrust. At this stage, parents must focus on meeting the wants and needs of their children so that trust and the knowledge that they are being loved is developed.

But when children become toddlers, they enter the stage of Autonomy versus Doubt. The search for autonomy is the search for independence. It is characterized by an "I can do it myself" attitude and a tendency to get into everything just because a toddler can! If you think about it, this is such an exciting time because everything is a new learning experience and adventure. For parents, the focus changes from meeting the needs of their babies to beginning to allow their toddlers to explore the world for themselves, all the while being vigilant to ensure that they are safe. Climbing on playground equipment is great, but climbing to the top of a piano to fly is just plain dangerous. A toddler's exploration for autonomy is the main reason parents find themselves saying "no" so often.

Toddlers are inquisitive, and using sign language enables them to expand their vocabulary, empowering them with more words, both signed and spoken, to talk about what they have found, to ask questions, or to express how they are feeling. Communication skills provide toddlers with autonomy because they can now tell you what they want. Signing provides toddlers with more usable words that allow for enhanced conversations and deeper understandings and more choices. Signed communication is a great way for a child to feel important and needed. Signing is a great way for your toddler to build a strong sense of autonomy.

The other side of the picture is doubt. This is the situation when children do not feel useful and are not allowed to contribute and therefore doubt their ability to be independent. This does not mean that parents must give children full reign so as to not damage their self-esteem. Instead what this suggests is that parents should be involved and give their children choices and experiences that enable them to be a contributing member of the household. HELP was described as an important sign earlier and is a wonderful sign for inclusion. You might ask for HELP around the house or HELP putting away toys. HELP gives children the sense that they are contributing. Other words like WHERE and WASH are useful when you ask, "WHERE did I put the keys?" and then let your child find them. Or, "Let's WASH the CLOTHES!" These are just a few examples of how you can encourage your helpful, enthusiastic toddler to be an important member of your family.

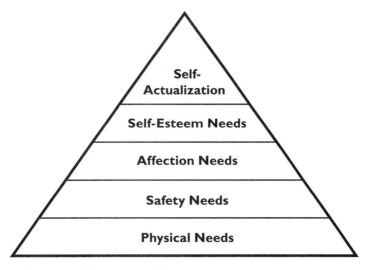

Maslow's Hierarchy of Needs
As you grow and your physical needs are taken care of, you
seek to satisfy other needs on the pyramid:
- Safety Needs—to know that you are safe
- Affection Needs—to know that someone cares about you
- Self-Esteem Needs—to know that you are doing a good job
- Self-Actualization—to reach your potential

Figure 3

Another psychologist, Abraham Maslow, created a Hierarchy of Needs. At the foundation of this pyramid is physical needs, which refers to having all your physical needs met—food, clothing, sleep, and comfort. For babies, these are the needs parents are working on the most. Maslow places the need for safety as the second step on the pyramid because once your physical needs are met, the next concern is for safety. This is why parents put safety locks on cabinets and in electrical sockets and expend so much energy watching out for the safety of their toddler. Again, signing won't diminish your concern, but it will provide you with silent behavior controls. Signing makes this easier because eye contact is required with your child. Children have to pay attention to see the signs. This allows you to engage your toddlers and communicate effective words like STOP, WAIT, GENTLE, CAREFUL, NO, WALK, HOT, AFRAID, SAD, and ANGRY (found in the glossary). While you have your child's focus and attention, you can explain matters of importance, or better yet, allow your child to understand what is being said.

Your Signing Skills

First you need to know and understand that you do not need any previous knowledge about American Sign Language or any signing skills to begin using sign language with your toddler. You will be learning ASL words, as many or as few as you wish, in conjunction with spoken English. As your child's understanding of these words grows, you can use signs to shape behavior, enhance communication and, as you will learn in part 3, have fun with signing activities that build vocabulary. You are not teaching or learning ASL as a second language. You are simply using the words and concepts of a structured language to expand your child's communication, silently shape behavior, and enhance cognitive development.

Learning signs is fun and easy to do. Most ASL signs are not complicated, and they often look like the word you are saying. You and your toddler can learn them together. Your commitment and enthusiasm will go a long way toward ensuring success for both you and your toddler.

Most parents come to acquire a good feeling about signing after about a month of using signs regularly with their toddlers. They usually become even more enthusiastic as they see the signing responses from their toddlers. It is a grand day indeed when you and your toddler are actually communicating with each other not only verbally but in sign language.

Your Toddler's Signing

Signing is such a natural activity for toddlers that they embrace it with enthusiasm. At this stage of physiological and mental development, their minds, eyes, hands, and bodies are ready to respond and learn through the use of ASL and its movement and visual characteristics.

Signing allows toddlers to playfully explore their world by combining their verbal skills with movements. It allows them to master and use lots of vocabulary and enables them to elicit many more responses from their parents and caregivers. This interaction helps them to learn and understand the meanings of a large collection of words. The combination of ASL and spoken English exposes toddlers to multiple ways to learn and to increase opportunities for additional synapses and dendrites, or connections, to be formed in their brains.

Tips for Successful Signing with Toddlers

Here are a number of ideas that you can use to greatly enhance your signing skills and the signing results you are striving to achieve. Signing can be kept very simple or expanded to include as many words as you wish to use, and by using the following signing concepts, you can become successful.

How Many Signs Do You Need to Learn?

You should begin with the number of signs that seems most comfortable for you. Our Jump Start on Smart section suggested focusing on six signs: STOP, GENTLE, HELP, HURT, CHANGE, and GOOD. Our goal with these words is to get you signing right away with words that help shape behavior, enhance communication, and develop empathy. But your toddler has the ability to learn lots of signs; therefore it is beneficial for you to expand your signing vocabulary as soon as possible. Later chapters will provide you with a wide variety of words and signing activities to increase your vocabulary. As you add signs choose those that not only meet your goals but are also of interest to your toddler.

Which Hand Should You Use?

Many signs require two hands, but many more can be formed by using one hand. Most people use their dominant hand as their primary signing hand. If you are left-handed, use your left, and if you are right-handed, use your right.

Sometimes, when signing with toddlers you don't have both hands free. In those situations you'll have to be creative and modify signs so that you can sign them with one hand. For example, LOVE can be signed with one hand or two hands across your chest.

Two-handed LOVE

One-handed LOVE

You can even switch hands. If you are holding your toddler's hand with your dominant hand and can't use that hand, sign the word with your other hand. Again the sign will have the same meaning.

EAT right-handed   *EAT left-handed*

Facial Expression and Body Language

Signs are enhanced by your facial expression and body language. Your facial expression can augment the meaning of a sign. For example, the word STOP

can be signed with very little expression saying, "Come on now, I'm asking you to STOP what you are doing." Or you can intensify the meaning with strong facial expressions saying, "STOP! Right now!"

STOP with strong facial expression.

Body language also demonstrates the meaning of a word. If you sign the word TIRED with very little body expression you are saying, "I'm TIRED." But if you sign it with lots of body expression you are saying, "I'm really TIRED!"

TIRED   *TIRED (with lots of body language)*

Toddlers find facial expressions and body language to be interesting and even humorous. An engaging smile combined with signing words demonstrates to toddlers that you are interested in them and the activity they are engaged in. Adding big eyes when signing about something big or a silly look when signing about something silly will encourage toddlers to pay attention and enjoy the playfulness of the activity.

Have Your Toddler's Attention

When signing with toddlers, it is important that they are at ease and that you have their attention. Is your toddler focused on watching you? Does your toddler appear ready to learn? If the answer to these questions is yes, then your toddler is ready to engage in signing with you. If, on the other hand, your toddler is distracted or not paying attention, then it is best to wait. When both of you are at ease and focused on one another, signing will be comfortable and fun and an activity to anticipate and engage in with pleasure.

Signs Need to Be Clearly Visible

Be sure you and your toddler can see each other when you are signing and that you are clearly forming each sign. To achieve this, arrange yourself so that you and your toddler are face to face, providing a clear line of sight. Use the traditional signing space by making all your signs at about the midchest level and up. You can be sitting side by side and still sign to each other as long as you and your toddler can turn to see the word that is being signed.

Speak and Sign Together

Speaking and signing words at the same time is important. Every time you say the word, sign the word. This gives the toddler the sound of the word as well as the picture of the sign. By simultaneously doing this, you are offering the word to the child through multiple senses. Your toddler will come to understand what a word sounds like, what a word looks like, and what a word feels like. This aspect of multiple sensory stimulation is one of the key reasons signing is so effective. There is no better way to introduce language to a child.

Speak Clearly

Clearly enunciate the word you are saying and signing. Always use good Standard English with your toddler. Pronounce words clearly and distinctly. Do not use what is commonly called "baby talk" and avoid exposing your child to cartoons or media products created for infants and children if these programs use poorly articulated words. Many cartoon characters do not speak clearly pronounced English. Be aware that children mimic the sounds of speech that they hear. That is why children often sound much like their parents. One of the best ways to help young children succeed in their future life is to help them acquire a strong vocabulary and good speech.

Use Correct Signs

Always sign the correct sign even though your toddler may sign something different. Try to consistently form each sign in the same, accurate manner every time you use it. When your toddler begins to sign to you, the signs will sometimes be immature or imperfect signs. This is absolutely normal. As toddlers continue to form signs, the signs will become clearer and more accurate. You can help them by never repeating their immature or personal sign. Rather, repeat the sign correctly and say the word that your toddler has just formed in an immature fashion. This reinforces the signing behavior and provides an additional example of the sign that your toddler can model.

Signing Success Story

One couple loved to take their son Joshua out to dinner on Friday nights. It had become a family activity that got them out of the house and doing something that they all seemed to enjoy. One of Joshua's favorite places was a pizza parlor. He loved cheese pizza. Joshua's parents also found that their son really enjoyed the atmosphere. The pizza parlor was a little noisy and provided structures to climb on and games to play. It was a place where he could enjoy himself and use up some of his exuberant energy.

Joshua's mother had been signing a variety of words with him and decided she would add PIZZA. It took no time at all for Joshua to connect his mother's sign to going out for pizza. He soon began to sign his version of PIZZA, a pointed finger movement that just kind of shook instead of making the letter Z with a P-shaped hand. Joshua's mother knew his meaning, kept signing it correctly and after a few months, Joshua moved from just shaking his finger to signing the Z with his index finger. His parents are sure he'll eventually sign PIZZA correctly. They've had fun watching him develop this sign, and Friday night pizza has become a family tradition.

PIZZA—Make the letter P with your right hand and draw the letter Z in the air.

Keep Signing Fun and Playful

It is so important that your signing activities always be fun and playful for toddlers. Never force them to sign. Encourage all their efforts to sign and reward them for being involved in signing. Your enthusiasm and support will foster a happy anticipation for signing and create a desire to engage in it often. Later in the book we will be offering you a wide variety of fun signing activities.

It is especially important that when you use these activities, you engage in them with attention, joy, and enthusiasm. Playful parental involvement is one of the most important gifts you can give toddlers to help them learn and grow.

Follow Your Child's Lead

In all your signing activities, whether you are signing while on a walk or around the house or with rhymes, songs, or accompanying stories, it is helpful for you to have a few signs that you know so you can easily move from one activity to another while continuing to sign. That way if you begin to sign a word in a book you are reading, but your child picks up another book to read, you can move to that book and sign the words you know. If you are outside signing and saying the name of an object, but your toddler points to or begins to sign another word, then move on and talk about this new area of interest. Knowing a variety of signs will enable you to easily move from one subject or activity to another.

Incorporate Signs into Your Daily Life

Signing and saying words you are using during the course of everyday events will help you to establish and reinforce signs and vocabulary that you and your toddler are using. With practice, signing will become second nature to you, and you will find yourself using signs with your words all the time.

To get started, use signs that help you find out what your toddler wants, or signs that will engage your toddler in an activity. Sign words you can regularly use. We have expressed to you that HELP is a wonderful engaging word. "HELP me with the car seat" or "HELP me carry something." You can combine words to teach lessons like STOP and LOOK. "Let's STOP and LOOK before we cross the street." Other engaging words can be used like this: "WHAT do you want to EAT or DRINK?" or "WHAT's that?" Be creative with signing and add words that you can include in your everyday conversation. You can find these signs and others in the glossary.

Create Special Times for Signing

You will find that the times you establish especially for signing activities will become anticipated events in your life. Create times for signing with songs, books, rhymes, and games. These activities help you to teach and use a wide variety of signs while providing you and your toddler with playful interaction. Again, part 3 will help you with this.

Relate Signs to Objects

When you make direct connections between signs and the objects they represent, you are enhancing the memorization and recall of these words. For example, at mealtime you can point to the cup and say and sign something like "That is a CUP. Would you like your CUP?" Or point to the cookie and say, "Would you like a COOKIE?" When you are outside, you can point to a wide variety of objects, sign and say the word, and encourage your toddler to sign with you.

CUP—Hold your left hand flat, palm up. Shape your right hand as if you are holding a cup, and then lift it. Repeat.

COOKIE—Hold your left hand flat, palm up. Curve the fingers of your right hand so your fingertips form a circle (as if holding on to the edges of a round cookie). Then touch your left palm twice, once directly on it and the second twisted slightly so it looks as if you are using a cookie cutter.

Signing the names for objects provides real benefits. It stimulates interactive communication between you and your toddler. It provides children with a much better chance of remembering the names of objects because they are using a variety of learning styles. And finally, it supports a toddler's language development.

Give Lots of Positive Reinforcement

Toddlers enjoy pleasing their parents. They love to get praise, and by giving them lots of positive reinforcement, you are encouraging them to engage in activities that they enjoy. When you positively reward their signing efforts every time they communicate to you with sign, you are fostering the desire in them to continue and do more. Success and rewards lead to more success and rewards. Children love to be cheered on.

Get Everyone Involved

It will be beneficial to toddlers if everyone around them signs, even just a little, and are aware of the signs that they are using. The more people who can interact and support your toddler's signing attempts, the better. This will also lead to more signs and more expressive and receptive vocabulary.

Caregivers and Grandparents

It is best if all your toddler's caregivers learn to use signs. Grandparents, family members, and others can learn the signs as you learn them. You can start out simply with the Jump Start on Smart signs (see chapter 4), or you can provide them with our 12 Everyday Signs to Use with Toddlers (found in the appendix) for them to refer to and use along with you.

However, sometimes this is not feasible. Some of the caregivers may feel uncomfortable using the signs, even if Mom or Dad is very enthusiastic about signing. As a result, the question sometimes facing parents is, "Should the others try to sign with my toddler?" The answer is that it is undoubtedly best not to force signing upon them if they are troubled about it. Often after the toddler starts to sign, and they notice the large vocabulary of words that the toddler rapidly develops, the other caregivers will have a change of heart and decide they want to sign with your toddler as well.

Toddler

It is good to encourage toddlers to help others with their signing. Ask them to demonstrate new words to older siblings or help teach a younger baby brother or sister to learn signs. You can even ask them to HELP you remember a word, though you know it, because not only does it help their recall but they also may be excited about teaching you something. All of these efforts will help to empower toddlers, to build their signing confidence, to enjoy signing activities, and to learn and remember more signs.

Siblings

If your toddler has older siblings, you can have the older children assist you in teaching the toddler how to sign words. This is an exciting and important activity for a brother or sister, who will feel needed and useful when introducing the ASL signs for English words to the youngest family member.

Often slightly older children are unable to actually help you with your toddler's care but if they know some of the ASL signs, they can teach their younger brother or sister. It is a helpful activity they can engage in with a good deal of competence. Allow them to shape your toddler's hand into the proper sign and move it to the correct location as long as they do this gently. Older siblings enjoy the opportunity to help care for your toddler and eagerly anticipate the prospect of interacting more fully with the toddler.

Conclusion

Mastering the basics is a growing activity. Some of our tips will come naturally to you and others you'll have to think about. Getting everyone involved in signing with your toddler helps to reinforce the use of sign and encourages your toddler to sign more. Add a few new signs at a time and be sure to sign and say each of the new words clearly, repeating them often during each day. Make signing a fun activity and create special times to sign with your toddler every day. Provide lots of positive reinforcement for all signing efforts and enjoy the enthusiasm your toddler develops for learning.

Chapter 6
More Signs

As we've written before, compared to signing with babies, signing with toddlers offers parents and caregivers greater flexibility in the quantity and types of signs that you choose. With so much room for choice, each parent can decide the direction to take, including how many or how few signs to use. Over the years, many parents have told us they believed that PLEASE and THANK YOU were very important signs for their toddler to learn. Others have said that signs like YES, NO, and WAIT were their choices because these signs helped them to shape their toddler's behavior. Still others wanted to focus on words that were of interest to their toddlers like BIRD, TRAIN, BOOK, and other vocabulary-building words.

The signs in this chapter are sorted into categories. Within each category are some signing suggestions along with additional words that you can find in the glossary. Pick and choose from these collections of signs the ones that you want to incorporate into your daily life.

Shaping Behavior

The following signs, CAREFUL, SHARE, YES, and NO, will help you shape your child's behavior as STOP and GENTLE did earlier in the book. Additionally requested signs like WAIT, QUIET, and COME can be found in the glossary of signs. Remember to use your facial expressions to reinforce the meaning of the words.

CAREFUL—Make the letter K with both hands and hold them in front, one hand above the other. Tap the little finger of one hand on the index finger of the other.

SHARE—Both hands are flat with thumbs up. They are turned slightly away from your body. Place your right hand at the base of the thumb and index finger on the left hand, and move it back and forth twice.

YES—Make the letter S with one hand, palm down, and then move it up and down (like a head nodding yes).

NO—Extend your thumb, index, and middle fingers. Hold your index and middle fingers up and together, and close your fingers to your thumb. Move your hand slightly down.

Maintenance

This next group of signs will help you with daily maintenance. Signs like BATH, BRUSH TEETH, MEDICINE, POTTY, and WASH will help you to communicate and reinforce the learning of these words and concepts.

BATH—Hold your fists, thumbs up, at the sides of your chest, then rub up and down repeatedly (as if you are washing your chest).

BRUSH TEETH—With your index finger extended from a fist hand and held by your mouth, imitate the movement of brushing your teeth.

MEDICINE—Hold your left hand flat, palm up. Make the number 5 with your right hand, bend the middle finger, place it on the palm of your left hand, then rock it side to side keeping the middle finger in place.

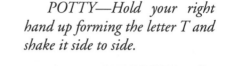

POTTY—Hold your right hand up forming the letter T and shake it side to side.

WASH—Make fists with both hands, right palm down and left palm up. Rub the right hand in a circular motion over the left hand. Repeat.

Immediate Needs

This group of signs that includes EAT, DRINK, BOTTLE, and SLEEP can help you and your toddler communicate some basic needs and wants. Knowing if your child is hungry and wants to eat or is thirsty and wants to drink can ease some of the frustrations your toddler feels when you do not understand. Start with these signs and later you can add others for words like HUNGRY, THIRSTY, TIRED, WAKE UP, and CUP.

EAT—Hold the thumb and fingertips of one hand together and bring your hand up to your mouth repeatedly (as if you are eating something).

DRINK—Shape your hand as if you are holding a glass, then bring it up to your mouth and tip it toward you so that it looks as if you're drinking from that glass.

BOTTLE—Lay your left hand flat, palm up. Set your right hand on it as if you are holding a bottle, then lift it up, squeezing your hand together, representing how it narrows at the top.

SLEEP—With your head bent, close your eyes and rest your cheek on the palm of your flat hand (as if you are pretending to be asleep). You may also encounter this as a two-handed sign (pictured) with both hands held together and under a cheek. Either version is fine.

Communication

The signs for ALL DONE, MORE, WANT, and WHAT can be used all day long to ask questions, to find out what your toddler might want or need. Additional signs in this category that you may want to add later include LOOK, LISTEN, AGAIN, SAY, ALL GONE, WHERE, and NOW.

ALL DONE / FINISHED —Hold up both hands with palms in, fingers at chest level, with palms flat and fingers loose. Then, in a quick motion, turn your palms so that they are facing out.

MORE—Hold the thumb and fingertips of both hands together (as you do with one hand for EAT) and then tap them together. Repeat.

WANT—Make the number 5 with both hands, palms up, held in front of your body. Move them toward your body and curve your fingers in.

WHAT—With your left flat hand facing right, draw a line with the index finger of your right hand across the fingers.

Courtesy and Affection

If you are signing I LOVE YOU, PLEASE, and THANK YOU every time you say them to your toddler, you will soon see these words returned. Additional signs GOOD NIGHT, GOOD MORNING, HUG, and KISS are often fun and useful.

I LOVE YOU—(shorthand, slang version) Hold your hand up near your shoulder, palm out, with your ring and middle fingers down, your index and little fingers up, and your thumb out. Keep this sign stationary; if you move it around, you'll be signing JET. Sometimes movement changes the meaning of a sign.

I / ME—Hold a fist up with your index finger out, and point it to the middle of your chest.

LOVE—Make fists, crossed at the wrist, and hold them against your chest (as if you are holding something you love).

YOU—Make a fist hand; point your index finger out and toward the person to whom you are talking.

PLEASE—Rub a flat hand, palm in, in a circular motion on your chest.

THANK YOU—Hold your right hand open, palm in, with your fingertips near your lips, and move it down and away, ending with your palm up.

Food Signs

Using signs at mealtime is a wonderful way to have your toddler's attention, connect signs to the objects they represent, and build signing vocabulary. These food signs will help you with this. Additional signs for words like ORANGE, CHEESE, CEREAL, and GRAPE are in the glossary.

APPLE—Make the letter X with one hand and place the knuckle of the index finger near the side of your mouth and twist it downward twice.

BANANA—Hold one index finger up, palm forward; then with the other hand, pretend you are peeling a banana from the top of your raised index finger down. The first motion is near the back of the index finger, and the second motion is near the front.

CARROT—Make the letter S with one hand and hold it by your cheek and snap it as if you are biting off a piece of a carrot.

COOKIE—Hold your left hand flat, palm up. Curve the fingers of your right hand so your fingertips form a circle (as if holding on to the edges of a round cookie). Then touch your left palm twice, once directly on it and the second twisted slightly so it looks like you are using a cookie cutter.

CRACKER—Hold your left arm bent and across your body. Make the letter A with your right hand, palm up; tap it near the elbow of your left arm.

JUICE—Sign the letter J by your cheek. Then add the sign for DRINK by shaping your hand like a cup and tipping it towards your mouth.

MILK—Squeeze your hand repeatedly (as if you are milking a cow).

WATER—Make the letter W with one hand and tap your index finger against your chin twice.

Objects

Using signs for objects that toddlers see and encounter on a daily basis and that are a big part of their lives will enhance the signing experience. You will find many more signs for objects in part 3 with the various activities, songs, stories, rhymes, and games that you can use with your toddler.

BLANKET—With both hands, imitate the movement of pulling a blanket up.

BOOK—Hold your flat hands together at chest level. Open your hands while keeping the little fingers touching (as if you are opening a book).

DOLL—Make the letter X with your right hand and brush the tip of your nose with the knuckle of your index finger. Repeat.

TEDDY BEAR—Cross your arms at your chest and scratch your fingers up and down repeatedly. This is the same sign as BEAR.

Clothing

Having a few signs for clothing that your toddler wears will provide you with additional ways to add signs into your life. "Let's get your COAT and HAT and go outside and play" or "Let's put on your SHOES and SOCKS before we go bye-bye" are just a couple of ways to do that. Additional signs for SHIRT and CLOTHES can be found in the glossary.

COAT—Make the letter Y with both hands. Hold them up near your shoulder and pull them inward to the middle of your chest (like you are pulling on a coat).

HAT—Pat the top of your head twice with a flat hand.

SHOE—Make the letter S with both hands, palms down and apart. Tap the sides of your fists together twice.

SOCK—With fist hands; extend your index fingers, palms down, and then rub the sides of your fingers back and forth.

Animals

As with object signs, you will find many more animal signs including BEARS, BIRDS, CATS, DOGS, FISH and more in the signing glossary. We will also use a number of animal signs in chapters 8 and 9 where they are included in activities. Here are a few animal signs that you can use to get started.

BUG—Make a fist and extend your thumb, index, and middle fingers. Touch your thumb to your nose and bend your index and middle fingers with a repeated movement.

HORSE / PONY—Make a fist with your thumb out and your index and middle fingers up. Hold the thumb at the side of your head, and bend your index and middle fingers up and down twice (like the ears of a horse).

PIG—Hold the back of a flat hand under your chin. Bend your fingers at the knuckles, and move them up and down twice.

TURTLE—Make the letter A with your right hand turned to the side, cup your left hand over the top, and wiggle your thumb (as if the head of a turtle was extended from its shell and wiggling).

Activity Signs

The signs in this category are for activities that you and your toddler can engage in every day. Use them to create special times to sign and with the activities in part 3. Additional signs to use with activities that you can find in the glossary are GAME and STORY.

PLAY—Make the letter Y with both hands, palms up, then twist them at the wrist to turn the palms up and down repeatedly.

READ—Hold your left hand up, your palm facing to the right. With the other hand, make the letter V, point the fingertips toward your left hand, and then move them from side to side and down (as if the right hand is reading words in a book).

SIGN—Make fists with both hands, extending the index fingers, and hold them pointing up. Then move your hands in large, alternating circles toward your chest.

SING / SONG—Extend your left arm with a flat palm. Swing your flat right hand back and forth on the left arm in a sweeping motion. Repeat.

Feelings

We discussed the importance of feeling signs earlier in the book. Here are the feeling signs most often used with toddlers along with words that are connected to feelings.

AFRAID—Make the letter A with both hands and hold them at each side of your chest with palms facing in. With a quick motion, open up both your hands, with fingers pointing toward each other. Your facial expression should reflect being afraid.

CRY—Bring both extended index fingers up to your face, palms facing in, and then move them down your cheeks, alternating sides, as if tears are rolling down your cheeks.

FEEL / FEELINGS—Make the number 5 with a bent middle finger. With your palm facing in, touch your middle finger to the center of your chest, and move it upward.

HAPPY—Hold your hands flat, palms in and thumbs up. Pat your chest in a circular motion. Use with a happy facial expression. Repeat.

MAD / ANGRY—Hold one hand up with the fingertips curved, palm in front of your chin. Then squeeze your fingers together just a little and move your hand slightly toward your chin. Use an angry facial expression.

SAD—Hold your hands flat, fingers spread and palms facing in, at eye level and then move them down a little. Use with a sad facial expression.

SILLY—Make the letter Y with one hand and hold it in front of your face. Twist at the wrist brushing your thumb across your nose. Repeat.

SMILE—Hold flat hands slightly bent, with your fingertips near the sides of your mouth. Then move your hands up each side of your cheeks (as if you are drawing a smile).

Family Signs

Here are signs that can be used for members of your family. The male signs, FATHER, GRANDFATHER, BOY, and BROTHER, are all signed at the forehead. This comes from the time when men and boys wore hats and the signs are placed where the brim of the hat would be. Female signs, MOTHER, GRANDMOTHER, GIRL, and SISTER, all begin at the chin because that is where the bonnets that women used to wear were tied. Additional signs for you to consider would be BROTHER, SISTER, BOY, and GIRL.

BABY—Fold your arms in front of yourself as if you are holding a baby, and rock them from side to side twice as if you are rocking a baby.

FATHER / DADDY— Make the number 5 hand with one hand, and touch your thumb to your forehead. Repeat.

GRANDFATHER— Make the number 5 hand with one hand, and touch your thumb to your forehead. Then gesture outward, tracing two arches in the air.

MOTHER/MOMMY—Make the number 5 with your hand and then tap your thumb on your chin. Repeat.

GRANDMOTHER—Make the number 5 with one hand and touch your thumb at your chin. Then move your hand outward, tracing two arches in the air.

Brother and Sister

Sometimes parents have found that brother and sister are a little more difficult and often will just use the manual letter B for brother and S for sister. The signs for brother and sister are found in the glossary.

B for brother

S for sister

Name Signs

Name signs have been used for many years. They are the signs people use to signify each other. Typically people do not make up their own name signs but rather they are given by other people. However, if you choose to use name signs, keep in mind these basic concepts.

Many name signs are the first initial of the person's name signed at the shoulder.

COREEN—Signed with a C at the shoulder.

Other name signs have the letter combined with a word sign that illustrates one of the person's specific characteristics. For instance, Marilyn's name sign, given to her by a Deaf ASL teacher, is the manual letter M sweeping across the palm in the sign for NICE. And Georgia was given the sign for GIRL as her name sign. You can also give name signs such as just a letter or part of a sign for any of your pets.

Conclusion

It is important to pick and choose only a few of the signs in this chapter to begin using with your toddler. Signing will help with communication, will encourage empathy, will provide for silent behavior control, and will build vocabulary. You can pick words that you want your toddler to learn along with others that you know your toddler will find interesting. Your toddler's ability to learn is rapidly growing and signing will enhance this process.

PART 3

Songs, Rhymes, Stories, Games, and Other Fun Signing Activities

Chapter 7
Signing Activities

Toddlers' language abilities are naturally expanding rapidly and parents can encourage this growth by providing toddlers with rich learning environments. These environments include being surrounded by good language models who offer clearly spoken words and sounds; language activities such as singing, reading, rhyming, and playing games that reinforce the meaning of words; and safe, supportive opportunities for toddlers to experiment with language on their own.

Signing activities enhance language growth and understanding by providing movement and visual reinforcement for words and their meanings. Toddlers can follow your lead, can attempt the words themselves, and even if their pronunciation is not clear, their signs will be. When engaging more than one toddler at a time, expand on our structure to engage all the children with you.

As you move into this section of the book keep in mind that as you and your toddler begin to explore various signing activities, it is the participation that is important and not the process of teaching signs. Toddlers need to embrace signing with enthusiasm and joy. Many of their views on signing will come from you. So, your involvement, your happy participation, your engaged attention, and your praise will encourage your toddler to become more and more involved.

Engaging Activities

Signing activities provide parents with great opportunities to interact and focus their attention on their toddlers. This focus not only helps to engage toddlers and build on their parent-child bonding, but it also helps to keep the toddler interested in the activity and to support and develop an enthusiasm for learning. Signing activities keep parents and children involved. Here are a few simple tips to remember for all the activities.

- Follow your toddler's lead and move from one activity to another.
- Stop an activity when your toddler wants to stop.
- Repeat activities whenever your toddler wants to do something "again."
- Provide activity choices. Allow your toddler to help direct what activity to do and where it leads you.
- Include signing activities in your toddler's daily routine.
- Be enthusiastic to encourage your toddler to participate and want to do more.
- Praise your toddler's efforts. Being supportive, involved, and encouraging is very important. GOOD is a wonderful sign that will help you reward efforts in all your activities. This was one of our Jump Start words in chapter 4.

Signing on a Walk

Often you will take walks or go to a park with your toddler. It is always fun to point out interesting sights as they come into view. Your toddler may be attracted to a CAT or a beautiful FLOWER or CAR on your outing. It is a good idea to name and sign at least three or four items you encounter on your walk. Here are three commonly used words, and more can be found in the signing glossary.

CAR—Make the letter S with both hands and palms facing toward each other, held at your chest. Imitate the movement of holding a steering wheel and driving a car.

CAT—Make the letter F using both hands, palms facing each other; hold them near the sides of your mouth, and pull outward as if you are tugging on the whiskers of a cat. Repeat.

FLOWER—Hold the fingertips of one hand together (as in the sign for EAT) and touch each side of your nose (as if you are smelling a flower).

Each of the items that you have selected to identify and sign for your toddler should be repeated and pointed out every time you are on your walk. Toddlers may not sign each of these signs back to you but soon will begin to understand that everything has a name and show a heightened interest in their surroundings.

If your toddler seems to pay particular attention to something seen on your walk, name this item and demonstrate the sign for it. In the event you do not know the sign, when you get home, look up the sign so you can connect the sign and word to the object the next time. If you have a picture of the object, you can then show it to your child and then say and sign the word, reinforcing what was seen on your walk. With continued use, soon your toddler will be repeating the sign for you.

Signing and Television

Television is part of most American children's homes and lives. It is used to entertain, to educate, and many times to simply baby-sit while parents get other tasks done. Ever since television was introduced, parents have struggled with its use. For years now, questions have continued to arise about how to use it, when to use it, how much to use it, what programming should be used, and more. The answers are personal to every family, but you should consider some of the upcoming ideas while making your determination.

Television will be a reality in the lives of most toddlers. They will be watching programs designed for them as well as being aware of television programs siblings and parents are watching. Each year hundreds of hours are spent watching television. This fact can't be ignored, but it can be used well.

Parents choose television as an activity for their toddlers for a variety of reasons. One of the main reasons is that parents see television as a valuable tool that can engage their toddler and support early learning. Television offers children ways to learn basic concepts and language. It helps them to understand feelings and values, and it provides children with knowledge about the world that is not available through everyday activities.

Another key reason parents choose television activities for their children is television's role as a baby-sitter. Parents often feel guilty about this and even look down upon using television in this way. The reality is that most parents will engage their children in programming that keeps their attention, for short periods of time, so that they can get other tasks or requirements done. In the past we used mobiles and blocks and other toys to keep children busy. Now we have an alternative called television that can be used, and it works. We believe in the responsible use of television activities.

Regardless of the reason a parent chooses to offer television as an activity, we believe that parental involvement is the most important part of television for toddlers. Television that is used responsibly can provide valuable learning experiences for toddlers. It offers wonderful images, interesting sounds and music, and experiences that toddlers would not have without television viewing and listening. It also provides a time for parents to interact with their toddler by engaging in conversations, activities, and signs for the images toddlers find interesting on television.

We believe these five considerations are important when choosing television programming for your toddler:

1. Consider whether or not the program is age appropriate for toddlers.
2. Watch the program with your toddler and observe whether or not the program is maintaining interest. Keep in mind that toddlers often engage in activities for short periods of time and move in and out of paying attention.
3. Interact with your toddler regarding action and characters that you see. Engage your child, point out objects, and talk about them.
4. Keep the activity fun and playful, laughing at silly scenarios that you both might see or experience.
5. Find ways to use the images, concepts, words, movements, or rhymes when your television is not on.

Quality signing DVD products and programs can use television to actively engage your toddler with images, music, and signs while reinforcing the vocabulary that you are trying to build. Television is also a good way for you and your toddler to learn signs together. These signs can then be worked into your daily life and into other fun activities. The *We Sign Play Time* and *Fun Time* DVDs provide parents of toddlers a wonderful signing, song, and interactive activity that can be shown and enjoyed over and over. In summary, choose quality television programming such as We Sign and others that encourage active participation, teach language in a fun and playful way, and energize your toddler to use the signs learned at other times during the day.

Your Signing Journal

A wonderful way to be involved in your toddler's signing is to keep a signing journal. You can incorporate this information into almost any of the predesigned books that are available to you in book and craft stores. You can also create your own journal by using blank art books that are available at stationary and art supply stores. It's always fun to add pictures and decorations to make each page become special. Visit www.signtospeak.com and use the log-in code STST109A to download free samples of journal pages.

Keeping a journal of your ongoing signing endeavors will be a rewarding experience. A clear, written record helps you know when you introduced a particular sign and when your toddler first used the sign. It also helps you to remember all the signs that your toddler has used, which words are of particular interest to your child, and which direction you may want your signing experience to go.

This written record will also help you retain wonderful memories. It will help you to recall precious moments in time and will provide you with written memories of events that often happen only once in a lifetime. Your journal will record fun moments, special signing events, favorite signing activities, and much more.

We have put together a list of topics that you can use to write about in your journal. Don't feel limited to just these topics. Write about any and all events and milestones you are interested in. Here are our suggestions to consider:

- Your child's name
- Your child's age when you began signing
- The first signs you used with your child
- The first sign your child signed to you
- Your child's age when this happened
- The story about how and when your child used this first sign
- Your feelings about your child's first signing experience
- Reasons you wanted to sign with your child
- Our special signing times
- The second word your child signed to you
- The story about how and when your child used this second sign
- Other favorite signs your child has learned to sign
- Stories about how and when your child began to sign these words
- Your favorite signs and reasons you liked them
- Mom's favorite signing memory
- Dad's favorite signing memory
- Other special signing moments with your child
- Your child's favorite song to sign
- Your child's favorite rhyme to sign
- Your child's favorite book to sign
- Your child's favorite word to sign
- Signing activities your child especially liked
- Your reflections on signing with your child as a toddler

These topics are to help you get started on keeping a journal or a written record of you and your toddler's signing activities. We encourage you to come up with your own ideas; you will find many signing stories to write about. Journals are a fun way to look back on experiences that you and your toddler had, along with fun memories that you can share for years to come.

For journal page downloads, see our Sign to Speak On-Line section at the end of the book.

Signing with Games

Signing games offer you and your toddler wonderful ways to playfully interact while gaining knowledge, expanding vocabulary, and exploring abilities. These games provide your toddler with not only a fun way to playfully interact but also a way to explore the world, learn language, understand concepts, and develop self-control and cooperation. Signing games help your toddler's concentration and encourage sharing with others. Signing games also allow toddlers the opportunity to manipulate their world as they change the rules or direction of the games.

Keep in mind that for teachers and caregivers it is very easy to adapt all these games for multiple children. The keys to successfully playing signing games with a group of children are

1. Engage all of them in the activity.
2. Sign all together or alternate between them.
3. Continue the activity until everyone has had the opportunity to participate.
4. To enhance the experience, have all the children say and sign the name of each object throughout the game.

The four words that are common to each of the games offered here are GOOD, YES, SIGN, and AGAIN. These words will allow you to praise, support, and direct the activities. Additional words can be found in the glossary.

GOOD—Hold your right hand flat, near your mouth, then move it down to your left hand, which is held with the palm up in front of you. Both palms will be facing up, with the back of your right hand on the palm of your left hand.

YES—Make the letter S with one hand, palm down. Then move it up and down at the wrist (like a head nodding yes).

SIGN—Make fists with both hands, extending the index fingers, and hold them pointing up. Then move your hands in large, alternating circles toward your chest.

AGAIN—Hold both hands bent and palm up. Move your right hand up and over until the fingertips are touching the palm of your left hand.

Signing games feature directed play—that is, play with rules. Rules provide for a structure on which the activities of the game will occur. For toddlers, the rules and structures should be simple and flexible. They should be seen as the foundation for future playing. Once any game's rules are understood, then you and your child can expand, change, and manipulate any game to fit your interests and desires.

Here are some guidelines to keep in mind before starting to use any of our signing games.

1. Learn the game prior to playing it.

2. Gather objects that you want to use.

3. Realize that toddlers have a very limited concept of following the rules. So be flexible and lenient.

4. Learn the signs that are to be used in the game.

5. Teach your toddler some of the signs that will be used in the game. If you are going to be connecting signs to objects, show the object and demonstrate the sign with the spoken word as you connect the sign to the object.

6. Always encourage your toddler to sign the signed words you are using in the game.

7. Choose a time to play the game, especially when you have your toddler's interest.

8. Keep the activity fun and playful and show genuine interest and pleasure to be participating with your toddler.

9. Since silliness is often a great way to encourage involvement, find ways to make silly mistakes. This will help you keep your toddler's attention, as most toddlers love to catch adults making mistakes. A simple example of this is that you can sign ELEPHANT when you say FROG. Wait for your toddler's reaction and then say, "NO, I made a SILLY mistake!" or "SILLY Mommy." Then go on and correct your error.

10. Have realistic expectations. Your toddler may sign only a few of the signs you are demonstrating. This is common. As your toddler becomes more comfortable with signing and their vocabulary grows, the number of signs they use will increase.

11. Play games or even parts of games over and over as your child's interest focuses on a certain activity. Toddlers gain knowledge through repetition.

12. Always give lots of positive reinforcement—signing GOOD is useful for this.

13. Never be forceful or coercive.

14. Follow up the games by using the signs from your game at other times during the day.

Signing Games

Here is a collection of signing games that you can play with your toddler. They are helpful in developing vocabulary as well as in learning how to follow directions and participate in social activities. These games are easy to learn and play. Once you are comfortable with a game's structure, then you can become creative and expand the games to cover other things of interest to you and your toddler. Detailed descriptions of signs are found in the glossary.

Game 1: Into the Box They Go!

A signing object box is simply a box that is filled with objects that you can use to encourage signing. These boxes can be anything from plain cardboard boxes that have been painted or decorated to toy boxes and metal containers. You can even create a variety of boxes filled with different objects that can be used in different games. For example, one can be an "animal box" with stuffed or toy animals, another could be a "color box" that has blocks of various colors, and another could be just a collection of objects. We suggest that for your first object box you focus on choosing items that are familiar to you and your toddler. The examples here feature common words. You can find them in the glossary.

This game is designed to help remember words and signs for objects and to reinforce the word HELP by providing a structured activity that allows your toddler to help you by putting items back into the box. Later you can use many of the same signs and make a fun game out of putting away the toys.

Preparation

Assemble an object box with six to ten items in it that are of interest to your child and for which you know the signs. For example, you could use a BALL, BANANA, BEAR, BIRD, CAR, FLOWER, FROG, HAT, JET, and PIG.

Concept
This game develops object, word, and sign recognition and encourages your toddler to sign the words for the objects from the box.

Keep in mind
Encourage your toddler not only to put the object away but to sign and say its name.

Signs
BALL, FROG, HELP, ALL GONE

Advanced signs
You can add the signs (found in the glossary) for SEE, INSIDE and NOW.

Setup
Empty objects from your signing object box onto the floor with the box in an accessible place so your toddler can put the objects back in.

Play the game
Choose objects, one at a time, and say and sign the name of each object as you put it away.

Dialogue *(sign the capitalized words)*
Do you see the BALL? SIGN BALL with me. GOOD!
HELP me and put the BALL inside the box. (Put the ball inside the box.)
Now the BALL is ALL GONE.

Do you see the FROG? SIGN FROG with me. GOOD!
HELP me and put the FROG inside the box. (Put the frog inside the box.)
Now the FROG is ALL GONE.

Repeat until all the objects are back in the box or your toddler's interest has changed. You can also sign the word SIGN in this game. (See the glossary.)

Be creative with this object box game. Once your toddler has demonstrated an understanding of the signed word, you can use only the sign for the object and not say the word in an effort to get a response to just the sign. "Do you see the BALL (silently sign the word)? Can you put the BALL (silently sign the word) into the box?" Another variation of this game would be to take the objects out of the box one at a time and sign the word for the object to each other after you place it on the floor.

ALL GONE

BALL

FROG

HELP

Game 2: What's That?

This is a game based on an activity that parents and toddlers engage in all the time. Toddlers often say "What's that?" as they point to objects for their parents to name. In this game, you are giving this activity some structure and supporting the memory and recall of the words by adding signs. You can play this game anytime and anywhere. Just point to the objects that you and your toddler both know the sign for and ask, "WHAT's that?"

Preparation
Collect objects that you and your toddler know how to sign. These could be toys of interest, objects from around the house, or items you are beginning to introduce signs for. For example, you could use a TEDDY BEAR or other stuffed animal and a JET or a CAR.

Concept
This game helps instill the sign for the word WHAT, a word all children will naturally say, and connect it to learning signs for objects.

Setup
Spread the objects out so that you can easily point to them. Be sure that both you and your toddler can easily see the objects.

Signs
WHAT, BEAR / TEDDY BEAR, JET

Play the game
Say and sign the name of each object. Here's a sample script:

Dialogue *(sign the capitalized words)*
WHAT's that? (Point at an object such as a teddy bear.)
Is it a TEDDY BEAR? YES, it is a BEAR, a TEDDY BEAR.
Can you SIGN TEDDY BEAR with me? (You and your toddler sign and say BEAR or TEDDY BEAR together.) GOOD!

WHAT's that? (Pointing to a different object such as a JET.) Is it a JET? YES, it is a JET. Can you SIGN JET with me? (You and your toddler sign and say JET together.) GOOD!

Repeat the same process for other objects until you have signed them all or your toddler's interest has changed.

Tip
As your toddler begins to connect the sign to the object, the structure of the game will change. You will say, "WHAT'S that?" while pointing to a bear and your toddler will sign BEAR. Remember to praise all signing efforts by signing GOOD! If you get to an object your toddler does not remember or know the sign for, then you would return to the original structure of the game.

Advanced
Once your toddler becomes comfortable with the structure of the game, you can take it with you everywhere. You can sign WHAT in connection to any words for objects you wish to teach. Getting your toddler to learn names for a wide variety of objects is the goal; signing WHAT adds a fun motion to the activity.

WHAT   JET   BEAR / TEDDY BEAR

Game 3: WHAT Does the Animal SAY?

This is a variation on game 2 and uses your toddler's natural inquisitiveness to foster the learning of signs for animals along with the sounds they make. Be sure to use the animal sign when you make the animal's sound. Extend the learning in this game by asking and signing what the animals say when you are reading animal books or when you encounter animals during other activities.

Concept
This game reinforces signs and words for animals.

Setup
Have your toddler's attention and sit facing each other.

Preparation
Learn the signs for six to ten animals that make sounds such as OWL, ELEPHANT, CAT, DOG, DUCK, FROG, and PIG. You will also need to know the signs for WHAT and SAY for this game.

Signs
WHAT, ELEPHANT, OWL, SAY

Play the game
Ask what sounds specific animals say. Say and sign the name of each animal and make the animal sign while making the animal's sound. Here's a sample script:

Dialogue (sign the capitalized words)
WHAT does an OWL SAY? WHOO, WHOO, WHOO. (You sign OWL when making the sound.)
Let's SIGN OWL. WHOO, WHOO, WHOO. (Encourage your toddler to sign OWL while making the sound.) GOOD!

WHAT does an ELEPHANT SAY? TOOT, TOOT, TOOT. (You sign ELEPHANT when making the sound.)
Let's SIGN ELEPHANT. TOOT, TOOT, TOOT. (Encourage your toddler to sign ELEPHANT while making the sound.) GOOD!

Repeat this process for other animals you or your toddler wish to sign.

Advanced
Ask your toddler, "What does the OWL (silently sign OWL) say?" Then sign and make the sound of the OWL. Do this for all the animals you know how to sign.

WHAT   OWL

SAY   ELEPHANT

Game 4: Stop and Wait

This is a game designed to help you create a structured way to interact and demonstrate to your toddler the meanings for the words STOP and WAIT. Once the meanings of these words have been learned, parents find them useful during the entire day to help shape behavior in a variety of situations. This game also includes action signs for activities that toddlers often engage in.

Concept
To reinforce the meanings of and signs for the words STOP, WAIT, and other action signs.

Setup
Have your toddler's attention and use a large play area where you and your toddler can move around.

Preparation
Learn the signs for STOP, WAIT, and other action words you want to use such as FLY, HOP, WALK, SLEEP, and RUN.

Tip
Have your toddler perform the action you say and sign. STOP and WAIT are key behavior-shaping signs and by adding them to this fun activity you make their understanding and use playful. Later you can have your toddler sign the action.

Signs
STOP, WAIT, HOP, WALK

Play the game
Say and sign each action. Here's a sample script:

Dialogue *(sign the capitalized words)*
Let's get ready to STOP…and WAIT. (Encourage your toddler to sign STOP and WAIT with you.) Can you HOP? (Encourage your toddler to sign HOP while he or both of you are hopping.)

Now STOP (pause) and WAIT (pause). (Pause for a few seconds while your toddler STOPS and then WAITS for the next sign.) GOOD!

Now can you WALK? (Encourage your toddler to sign WALK while he or both of you are walking.)

Now STOP (pause) and WAIT (pause). (Pause for a few seconds while your toddler STOPS and then WAITS for the next sign.) GOOD!

Repeat these steps for each additional action you and your toddler do.

Advanced
Only sign and don't say the action words you want your toddler to respond to.

STOP

WALK

HOP

WAIT

Conclusion

Games can provide great ways to be creative while expanding your and your toddler's signing abilities. Because signing is an activity in which all children can be successful, these activities can be used by caregivers and teachers that have several toddlers or even varied ages of children. Games allow you to modify the rules, change the signs, and vary the objects that you use. You can combine the rules or concepts from two or more games together into a new activity that can be even more enjoyable for you and your child. The games help your toddler to expand vocabulary, develop self control, and understand concepts, and they also encourage cooperation. Signing games provide quality parent-child interaction that reinforces your toddler's knowledge of words and provides you with a silent and effective communication skill that you will use throughout your everyday life.

Chapter 8
ABCs, Books, and Storytelling

When you add signing to learning of the alphabet, reading books, and telling stories, you are enhancing your toddler's language development. Signing provides parents and teachers with another dimension that, when added to these activities, increases your toddler's involvement, participation, and language understanding, and provides for pleasurable and entertaining interaction.

Try to make signing a habit. Even though we have suggested you gain your toddler's attention first, this will not always be possible. Sometimes when your child is clearly focused on you, a noise may occur or another person may enter the room. Your child will be attracted to the new stimulus and cease paying attention to you. When this happens, do not be stressed. Continue to sign and speak. If you are consistent, patient, and calm, your toddler will soon be signing back to you. We do not know of any toddler that didn't eventually begin to sign if the parents stuck with it. So do make it a habit. Detailed descriptions of signs are found in the glossary.

Alphabet Finger Play

American Sign Language has a manual alphabet that assigns each of the 26 letters of the English alphabet a one-handed sign. The manual alphabet is found in our glossary. You can begin to show your toddler some or all of the letters when reading or looking at picture books in the evening before bedtime. ABC picture books usually focus on one subject, such as animals, and tend to pair a picture of a letter with a picture of an animal that has a name that begins with that letter.

Young toddlers will generally be able to sign only a few of the simplest letters. They are still developing the manual dexterity needed. When they are 3 years old, their fingers have usually grown and developed sufficiently for them to be able to form most of the letters. Learning the ABCs with sign can become a wonderful finger-play activity. When you read an alphabet picture book, indicate the printed letter and show them the manual sign for the letter.

For toddlers, an easy letter to begin with is C, and many times, particularly in animal books, the letter C is associated with cow. COW is an easy sign for children to make. It represents the horns on a cow and children have fun making the sign. You will have multiple opportunities to use C with other signs, for example, C is for CAT or C is for CUP or C is for CAR. (All of these signs can be found in the glossary.) You are reinforcing the letter, a word, and the sound of that letter, all at the same time.

C

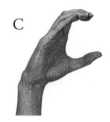

COW

CAT

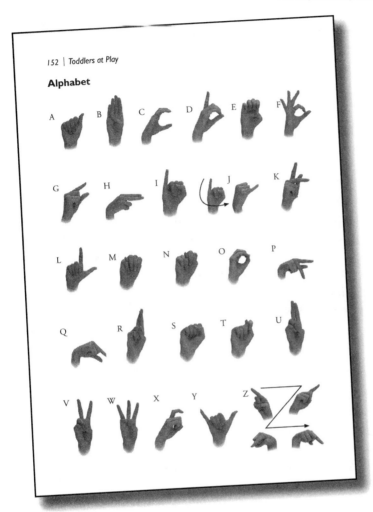

152 | Toddlers at Play

Alphabet

The alphabet from the glossary—see p. 152.

When you start to introduce the manual letters, begin with just one letter. There are several reasons to start with the letter C when you begin to teach your toddler to use the American manual alphabet. One aspect that is difficult for most children is the fact that there are upper and lower case letters and in most cases they look very different. However, an upper case letter C and a lower case letter c are the same shape; they are simply different sizes, and that makes recognizing them a much simpler task.

Additionally, when children form the letter with their hand, it also looks like the printed letter C. Although it is backward, unless the child is left-handed, children do not seem to be troubled by this. But, if any children notice the C looks backward, you can have them form the sign in front of a mirror, and the C will look perfect.

When toddlers are easily able to find a letter C, you can introduce other letters like A and B. What is occurring in a child's body and brain is amazing. Children who can identify a letter visually, form the letter manually, and say the letter, also know the letter visually, kinesthetically, and orally. Toddlers are acquiring knowledge through multiple senses. In addition, at the same time this happens, unseen by the human eye, children are establishing multiple important synapses in their brains.

This early training with the manual alphabet will be a terrific aid to children. When they begin to learn to read they will rely on their knowledge of letters to decipher print. If they have had this early playful experience with manual letters, learning to read will prove far less daunting for them when the time arrives. Their knowledge of the manual alphabet will move them down the road to reading readiness.

Signing with Books

Reading books to children is an activity that is an anticipated pleasure for both parents and children. Many parents find a joy in sharing this quiet time with their child as they often recall similar experiences they themselves had during their earlier childhood days. Those who absolutely love words cannot think of anything they would rather do with their toddler than read or tell stories and share their enthusiasm for literature.

For parents who are not quite as fond of reading activities, it is important to understand that reading to your child is a significant step and needed for a child's strong academic development. For such a parent, adding signs to the reading experience can often make the reading process more appealing. Reading when signing is included, even in a minimal manner, involves more action and physical movement.

When you sit down to read a book with your toddler, you will usually use only a few signs that represent a main idea from the book. For instance, a wonderful book used often with toddlers is *The Little Engine That Could*. A few signs lend themselves well for use with this book. The Little Engine is the main character in this book, so most moms and dads will sign TRAIN whenever they say engine. The other words that are frequently used with this story are THINK and CAN. Sign TRAIN, THINK, and CAN each time you read them in the book.

TRAIN—Make the sign for the letter U with both hands, holding your palms down. Lay the fingers of your right hand on top of the fingers of your left. Then move the right-hand fingers back and forth on the left-hand fingers. Repeat.

THINK—Double tap the side of your forehead with your pointed index finger.

CAN—Make the letter S with both hands and hold them, palms facing down, in front of your body. Move them downward a short distance. Repeat.

You can use signing with any number of other books. For example, now that your toddler knows TRAIN, you can also use it with Thomas the Tank Engine books. You can learn RAINBOW and FISH for signing with The Rainbow Fish, learn BEAR to sign with any of the Corduroy Bear books, DOG for Clifford books and even BIRD for Big Bird books.

RAINBOW—Make the number 4 with your right hand and move it from your left shoulder in an arch over to your right shoulder.

FISH—With a flat hand, mimic the movement of a fish as it swims.

BEAR—Cross your arms at your chest and scratch your fingers up and down repeatedly.

DOG / PUPPY—With a flat hand, tap the side of your hip. Then bring your hand up and snap your fingers.

BIRD—Hold your right hand by your mouth, with your index finger and thumb pointed out. Open and close these fingers, imitating the movement of a bird's beak.

Storytelling with Signs

Storytelling has been part of our human experience since language was developed and has been used to pass along traditions, culture, history, values, morality, and more from one generation to the next for thousands of years. It is an activity that everyone is capable of incorporating into daily life. If you think about it, we tell stories all day long. We tell about our weekend's activities to people we work with, we recount family history to children and to other family members, and we describe our life's experiences to our friends.

Storytelling provides many benefits to toddlers. It allows their imaginations to bloom and grow as they create their own images of the characters, events, and environments instead of looking at the images that are printed for them in books or shown on television. Storytelling provides them with an activity that will expand vocabulary, develop an enjoyment of language, and engage their listening skills. Storytelling enables them to remember sequencing of events, comprehend meanings, and recall what they have learned.

You as the Storyteller

When you tell stories there are 10 simple rules that will help you.

1. Choose a simple story to tell. Often the best stories to start with are ones with which you are very familiar.
2. Learn the story, its parts (the beginning, middle, and the end), its important events, problems, and conflicts.
3. Tell the story to yourself and picture it in your head.
4. Learn the characters and give them personalities. For example, a big bear could be represented by puffing out your chest and sitting taller or by making your voice deeper and louder. You can depict the bear as mean, nice, scared, happy, or sad by the look on your face.
5. Always tell the story in your own words. Storytelling is not memorization.
6. Learn the signs for a few key words that are repeated in the story. Add more words as you and your toddler become comfortable signing the key words.
7. Have your toddler's attention when telling the story.
8. Encourage your toddler to participate in the signs.
9. Praise and reward all your toddler's signing efforts.
10. Tell the story often so that your toddler will look forward to signing it with you. Remember that toddlers love repetition.

Stories for You to Tell

We have chosen the following very popular stories that toddlers enjoy for you to tell and sign. Each of the stories feature suggested signs. Descriptions of these signs along with additional ones can be found in the glossary. Keep in mind that you do not have to sign all the words we are suggesting. You can choose one or two to start with and then add others as you go along. Picture books of all of these tales can be found easily, so you can also sign along as you tell the story with pictures as well. Look to the glossary for detailed signing instructions.

The Little Red Hen

Tips
Try to give the DUCK, CAT, and DOG different voices.

Signs
BIRD/HEN/CHICK, CAT, DOG, DUCK, EAT, HELP, YES, NO

Once there was a Little Red HEN who was scratching in the farmyard when she found a grain of wheat.

HEN

"Who will HELP me plant the wheat seed?" she asked.

"NO, not I," said the DUCK.

"NO, not I," said the CAT.

"NO, not I," said the DOG.

"Very well then," said the Little Red HEN, "I'll plant it myself." So she planted the grain of wheat.

DUCK

After a while, the wheat grew tall and ripe.

"Who will HELP me cut the wheat?" asked the Little Red HEN.

"NO, not I," said the DUCK.

"NO, not I," said the CAT.

"NO, not I," said the DOG.

"Very well then, I will," said the Little Red HEN. So she cut the wheat.

CAT

When she was finished she asked, "Now, who will HELP me thresh the wheat?"

"NO, not I," said the DUCK.

"NO, not I," said the CAT.

"NO, not I," said the DOG.

"Very well then, I will," said the Little Red HEN. So she threshed the wheat.

When the wheat was all threshed, she asked, "Who will HELP me take the wheat to the mill to have it ground into flour?"

"NO, not I," said the DUCK.

"NO, not I," said the CAT.

"NO, not I," said the DOG.

"Very well then, I will," said the Little Red HEN. So she took the wheat to the mill herself.

When the wheat was ground into flour, she said, "Who will HELP me make this flour into bread?"

"NO, not I," said the DUCK.

"NO, not I," said the CAT.

"NO, not I," said the DOG.

"Very well then, I will," said the Little Red HEN. So she took the flour, turned it into bread, and baked it in the oven until is was a beautiful loaf of golden brown bread.

When the bread was all done, she asked, "Who will HELP me EAT this beautiful loaf of bread?"

"YES, I will EAT the bread!" said the DUCK.

"YES, I will EAT the bread!" said the CAT.

"YES, I will EAT the bread!" said the DOG.

"NO, you will not EAT this bread with me!" said the Little Red HEN. "You did not HELP me plant it, cut it, thresh it, mill it, or turn it into bread. You will now not get to EAT it with me."

So the Little Red HEN called to her CHICKS who all came running up quickly and they all ATE the bread with their mother, the Little Red HEN.

DOG

HELP

EAT

NO

YES

Advanced

These are additional signs you can use when reading or telling this story: I, LITTLE, RED, SAY (for said), ALL DONE, FINISHED (found in the glossary).

Goldilocks and the Three Bears

Tips

Give the characters different voices, such as a deeper voice for papa and a higher voice for baby. You can start out with just a few signs like BEAR, GIRL, and GOOD. Add other signs as you build them into your vocabulary.

Signs

BEAR, Goldilocks (sign GIRL), EAT/TASTE, HOT, COLD, SLEEP/BED, SAT, Just Right (sign GOOD), PORRIDGE

Once upon a time there were three BEARS who lived in a little house in the forest. There was the Big Papa BEAR, with a big papa BEAR voice; the middle-sized Mama BEAR, with a middle-sized voice; and the cute little Baby BEAR, with a little squeaky voice.

BEAR

One morning the three BEARS sat down to EAT some PORRIDGE for breakfast. When Papa BEAR TASTED his PORRIDGE, he said, "This PORRIDGE is too HOT." When Mama BEAR TASTED her PORRIDGE, she said, "This PORRIDGE is too HOT." And when Baby BEAR TASTED his PORRIDGE, he said, "This PORRIDGE is too HOT." The three BEARS decided to go for a walk and let their PORRIDGE cool down.

EAT

A little while after the BEARS had left, a little GIRL named Goldilocks came upon the house. She walked up to the door and knocked. She waited, but no one answered. So Goldilocks (GIRL) opened the door and walked inside.

She saw, there on a table, three bowls of PORRIDGE—a big bowl, a middle-sized bowl, and a little bowl. She went up to the big bowl, TASTED it, and said, "This PORRIDGE is too HOT." She went to the middle-sized bowl of PORRIDGE, TASTED it, and said, "This

PORRIDGE

PORRIDGE is too COLD." She went to the little bowl of PORRIDGE, TASTED it, and said, "This PORRIDGE is just right (GOOD)!" She then ATE it all up.

When she finished, she saw that there were three chairs in the next room—a big chair, a middle-sized chair, and a little chair. She SAT in the big chair and said, "This chair is too hard." She SAT in the middle-sized chair and said, "This chair is too soft." She then SAT in the little chair and said, "This chair is just right (GOOD)." Then suddenly, the chair broke.

She then walked up some stairs and saw three BEDs—a big BED, a middle-sized BED, and a little BED. She was tired, so she decided to go to SLEEP. She lay down on the big BED and said, "This BED is too hard." She then went to the middle-sized BED, lay down, and said, "This BED is too soft." She then went to the little BED, lay down, and said, "Yes, this BED is JUST RIGHT (GOOD)," and she went to SLEEP.

A little while later, the three BEARS returned home to EAT their PORRIDGE. When Papa BEAR looked at his PORRIDGE, he said, "Someone's been EATing my PORRIDGE." Then Mama BEAR looked at her PORRIDGE, and said, "Someone's been EATing my PORRIDGE." Finally, Baby BEAR said, "Someone's been EATing my PORRIDGE, and it's all gone."

So the three BEARS walked to the next room. Papa BEAR said, "Someone's been SITting in my chair." Mama BEAR said, "Someone's been SITting in my chair." And Baby BEAR said, "Someone's been SITting in my chair, and it's all broken."

So the three BEARS walked up the stairs to the bedroom. Papa BEAR then said, "Someone's been SLEEPing in my bed." Mama BEAR said,

HOT

GIRL

COLD

SAT

"Someone's been SLEEPing in my bed." And finally Baby BEAR said, "Someone's been SLEEPing in my bed and she's still here!"

GOOD

With the sound of Baby BEAR'S squeaky little voice, Goldilocks (GIRL) woke up, jumped out of BED, ran down the stairs, out of the house, and through the forest as fast as she could go. Where did she go? No one knows, but the three BEARS never saw her again.

Advanced

These are additional signs you can use with this story: FATHER/PAPA, MOTHER/MAMA, BABY, WAIT, WALK, ALL DONE, RUN/RAN, AWAKE/WAKE UP, CHAIR, TIRED.

SLEEP/ BED

Three Little Pigs

Tips

Be sure and give the WOLF a different voice in the story. A deeper and meaner voice always adds to the fun of this tale. You can choose as few or as many signs as you wish to use in the story.

Signs

PIG, HOUSE, ALL DONE/FINISHED, DANCE, SING/SONG, BLOW, MAD, NO, WOLF, HOT.

PIG

Once upon a time there were three little PIGS. One day their mother told them they had to go out on their own, build their own HOUSEs, and seek their own fortunes.

The first little PIG decided to build his HOUSE out of straw. He quickly FINISHED and went outside where he DANCED and SANG.

HOUSE

The second little PIG decided to build his HOUSE out of sticks. He quickly FINISHED and went outside where he DANCED and SANG.

The third little PIG decided to build a strong HOUSE. He built his HOUSE out of bricks, and it took a long time to FINISH. He knew his brothers FINISHED quickly and were DANCING and SINGING, but he also knew that when he was ALL DONE, he would have a good strong HOUSE.

One day along came a WOLF. He stopped at the HOUSE of the first little PIG. It was made out of straw. The WOLF said to the little PIG, "Little PIG, little PIG, let me come in."

The first little PIG said, "NO, NO! Not by the hair on my chinny, chin, chin!"

Then the WOLF said, "Then I'll huff and I'll puff and I'll BLOW your HOUSE down." So he huffed and he puffed and he blew (BLOW) the little straw HOUSE down.

The first little PIG ran quickly to the HOUSE of the second little PIG. After a while, the WOLF came along and stopped at the HOUSE built of sticks and said, "Little PIG, little PIG, let me come in."

The second little PIG said, "NO, NO! Not by the hair on my chinny, chin, chin!"

Then the WOLF said, "Then I'll huff and I'll puff and I'll BLOW your HOUSE down." So he huffed and he puffed and he blew (BLOW) the little stick HOUSE down.

The two little PIGs then ran to the HOUSE of the third little PIG. After a while, the WOLF came along and stopped at the HOUSE built of bricks. He said, "Little PIG, little PIG, let me come in."

The third little PIG said, "NO, NO! Not by the hair on my chinny, chin, chin!"

Then the WOLF said, "Then I'll huff and I'll puff and I'll BLOW your HOUSE down." So he huffed and he puffed and he blew (BLOW) and he huffed and he puffed and he blew (BLOW) and he

ALL DONE

DANCE

SING

WOLF

NO

BLOW

huffed and he puffed and he blew (BLOW) but he could not BLOW the brick HOUSE down.

MAD

The WOLF got very MAD and decided to go down the chimney to get into the HOUSE. The little PIGS saw what he was trying to do, so they put on a big pot of boiling HOT water in the fireplace. The WOLF came down, but when his tail touched the HOT water, he said, "Ouch! That hurts!" He ran up the chimney, across a big field, and into the woods. To this day the three little PIGS DANCE and SING and have never seen the WOLF again.

HOT

Advanced

These additional signs can be used and are found in the glossary: DOWN, UP, FIRST (use number 1), SECOND (use number 2), THIRD (use number 3), CHIN, SAY/SAID, HURT, MOTHER, WATER.

Conclusion

When you use signs with spoken letters to help your toddler learn the alphabet or with spoken words when you are telling stories, you enhance the interaction between you and your toddler while providing language-rich learning activities. When introducing the alphabet, start with one letter at a time and introduce more as your child begins to recognize the letters and sign them back to you. Also, because of the stage of physical development, begin with the easy letters to sign such as C or A. When you are telling stories to your toddler, select stories that you are familiar with and sign just a few of the key words. You can add more as your toddler participates in the signing of the story with you. Remember to give the characters personalities and even different voices to keep the story interesting and fun. The alphabet and storytelling activities help toddlers to build strong language and decoding tools that provide reading readiness foundations.

Chapter 9
Rhymes and Songs

Parents, caregivers, and teachers use rhymes with their toddlers as a form of play. Rhyming is interactive and generally familiar as part of every adult's own childhood. Traditional Mother Goose nursery rhymes are timeless favorites. They have well-known words and melodies. However, other rhymes, once learned, provide the same intrinsic pleasure and comfort when parents share with toddlers.

Rhymes are generally short and simple and are often silly.

However there is more to rhyming than just being a fun and engaging activity. Rhymes also play an important part in early learning. They provide toddlers with the foundations for a love of reading as they learn to recite rhymes "by heart" before they can read the words. Rhymes enable toddlers to begin to learn about words, letters, and sounds. Rhymes help them to anticipate sounds and become familiar with similar sound patterns that will aid them later in decoding words as they are learning to read.

Signing with Rhymes

When you add signing, you provide toddlers with an activity that involves a variety of learning styles as we discussed in chapter 2. You can choose to say, sing, or chant rhymes while you are signing them. Here are some tips to help you:

- Sign only a few words and add more as you and your toddler become better at signing.
- Practice the rhymes and signs before you introduce them to your child.
- Teach a few signs to your toddler ahead of time.
- Be actively and enthusiastically engaged in the activity. Use your voice, body language, and facial expressions to enhance each rhyme.
- Repeat the rhymes as often as your toddler is interested in doing so.
- Use the signs learned in the rhymes all day, in conversation and in other activities.
- When you have several toddlers (or even a mixed age group of children), be sure all children can clearly see you and the signs so that all can participate.
- Praise and reward your toddler's efforts.

Rhymes for You to Sign

We have selected the key words for you to sign in each of the following rhymes. You can choose to use them all or pick just a few to begin with and add other signed words later. Look over the tips before you begin, as they will help you to sign and be creative with each of the rhymes that follow. Look for detailed signing information in the glossary.

I Went Outside One Day

You can easily be creative with this rhyme by adding more verses featuring other animals. Use the sign for the animal when you are making its sound. Additional signs for animals along with signs for I, SAW and SAY can be found in the glossary.

I went OUTSIDE one day.
Saw a HORSE along the way.
The HORSE said Neigh, Neigh, Neigh.
YES, that's what the HORSE did say.

I went OUTSIDE one day.
Saw a MONKEY along the way.
The MONKEY said Ook, Ook, Ook.
YES, that's what the MONKEY did say.

OUTSIDE   HORSE

MONKEY   YES

Mommy Says I Love You

Be creative by changing "Mommy" to "Daddy" or "Grandma" to "Grandpa" or to any other family member. You can also change the animals you wish to use. Use the sign for the animal when you are making its sound. You can find additional signs to use in the glossary.

The little LAMB says Baa, Baa, Baa.
The little COW says Moo, Moo, Moo.
The little HEN says Cluck, Cluck, Cluck.
And Mommy says I LOVE YOU!

The little CAT says Meow, Meow, Meow.
The little OWL says Whoo, Whoo, Whoo.
The little PIGGY says Oink, Oink, Oink.
And Mommy says I LOVE YOU!

SHEEP/LAMB   COW

HEN/BIRD   I LOVE YOU

CAT   OWL   PIG

It's Time to Go to Sleep

Sometimes ASL signs represent concepts. For example, in this rhyme you will sign SLEEP for the word sleep as well as for the word bed, and for "sleepy head." Sign SLEEP on one side of your face and BED on the other. This rhyme is made even more enjoyable when you change the animals to those you or your toddler choose to sign (additional signs are found in the glossary).

It's time to go to SLEEP.
It's time to go to BED.
It's time for you to CLOSE your EYES.
And lay down your SLEEPY head. [*sign SLEEP*]

Go to SLEEP big ELEPHANTS.
Go to SLEEP DUCKS, too!
Go to SLEEP all FISH and BUNNIES.
Now SLEEP my darling YOU.

SLEEP/BED   ELEPHANT

DUCK   YOU   CLOSE EYES

BUNNY/RABBIT   FISH

Mother Goose Nursery Rhymes have been used with children for over 300 years. They are one of the oldest and most widely used parts of our oral language tradition. These rhymes are not only very well known, but they provide toddlers with simple and fun ways to learn about letter sounds, understand words, and enjoy the rhythm of language, and they are often the first introductions children receive about music and song. Mother Goose Nursery Rhymes are short word plays that can be silly with meanings long lost, as well as full of messages meaningful to young children.

Row, Row, Row Your Boat

Continue to sign BOAT when saying the line "Gently down the stream." You can add additional actions to the song for toddlers to sign and do, like FLY, WALK, HOP, or RUN. For example, you can say "Fly, fly, fly away, high up in the sky. Fly, fly, fly away, high up in the sky."

Row, row, row your BOAT
Gently down the stream. [*sign BOAT for this line*]
MERRILY, MERRILY, MERRILY, MERRILY
Life is but a DREAM.

BOAT

HAPPY/MERRILY   DREAM

Peas Porridge Hot

Be sure and use lots of facial and body expressions when signing HOT and COLD to make the activity fun and interesting and support the learning of the sign and meaning. Be creative by changing the words to COOKIES and CRACKERS or CHEESE and CARROTS. These and the sign for OLD can be found in the glossary.

Peas PORRIDGE HOT,
Peas PORRIDGE COLD.
Peas PORRIDGE in a pot,
nine days old.

Some like it HOT,
Some like it COLD.
Peas PORRIDGE in a pot,
nine days old.

CEREAL/PORRIDGE

HOT

COLD

Twinkle, Twinkle Little Star

The sign for YOU in this rhyme is a directional sign. YOU refers to the star, so the sign is pointed up like you are pointing to a star. When signing TWINKLE, alternate hands. Additional signs you can add are WORLD, WHAT, LITTLE, and ABOVE (found in the glossary).

TWINKLE, TWINKLE, little STAR
How I WONDER what YOU are.
Up above the world so HIGH,
Like a DIAMOND in the SKY.
TWINKLE, TWINKLE, little STAR,
How I WONDER what YOU are.

TWINKLE   STAR

WONDER   YOU (to the star)   HIGH

DIAMOND   SKY

Little Miss Muffet

This rhyme has a variety of concepts. AWAY is a variation on the sign RUN AWAY to develop the meaning of RUN AWAY as it reflects the concept that Little Miss Muffet is running away. For "little," as in "Little Miss Muffet," you will sign CHILD because "little" in this case represents a child. SPIDER SITS adds the movement of sitting to the sign for SPIDER. You can expand on this by moving the sign for SPIDER to a sitting position by your side, reflecting the concept of "sits down beside her." You can also simplify the signs to fit your comfort level, and you add signs for CHAIR/TUFFET and CURDS and WHEY / CEREAL (found in the glossary).

LITTLE [*sign CHILD*] Miss Muffet SAT on her TUFFET
EATing her curds and whey.
When along came a SPIDER who
SAT [*sign SPIDER SITS*] down beside her
And FRIGHTENED Miss Muffet AWAY [*sign RUN AWAY*].

CHILD

SIT/SAT

EAT

SPIDER

FRIGHTENED/ FEAR

RUN AWAY

Signing with Songs

Songs, as part of the human experience, predate written language and are at the heart of humanity. All people everywhere in the world create music and have used it for passing on traditions, teaching lessons, telling of history, bonding socially, and much more, for thousands of years.

Songs have many positive effects on children. Singing songs is a fun and playful way to learn vocabulary and rhyming and to interact with others. When combined with movement, singing has proven to be a powerful memory and recall activity. In fact, most of us have firsthand experience with this. We have learned finger plays, jump rope songs, and other action-oriented songs as children and can still firmly recall them as adults. When we add sign language to songs, we are adding movement and visual components that offer children a powerful way to remember receptive and expressive vocabulary.

Tips for Signing with Songs

Singing songs with toddlers is easy. They do not judge your singing critically. Instead, they enjoy the interaction, the language, rhyme, melody, and the comfort of a parent's voice. Parents, teachers, and caregivers do not need exceptional singing or signing abilities to enjoy these songs with toddlers. All you need is the desire to have fun. Here are some simple guidelines:

- No singing experience is necessary to have fun with this activity. The sound of your voice (singing, chanting, or talking) is what your toddler loves to hear.
- Learn the words and melody of the song ahead of time. (Visit www.signtospeak.com, use the log-in code STST109A, and you can listen to, download, and view videos of all the songs featured in this book.)
- Learn a few key signs in the song. Start with these signs and add more as you become comfortable.
- Have your toddler's attention. Be sure that your child is focused on you and what you are doing.
- Follow your toddler's cues. If attention begins to waver, change the song, be more enthusiastic, encourage participation, or change the words to regain her focus.
- Be enthusiastic as you sing and sign each song.
- Make the experience interactive by stopping at each sign and encouraging your toddler to sign with you.

- Keep the activity fun and playful. The adult-child interaction and involvement is what is important.
- Incorporate the signs from the songs in conversation and in different situations throughout the day.
- Praise and reward all of your toddler's efforts to participate with you.

Singing and signing is fun and engaging. It is an activity that bonds parents and toddlers together and, once learned, is an activity that can be participated in almost everywhere. Finally, the sign for SING is the same for SONG.

SING / SONG—Extend your left arm with a flat palm. Swing your flat right hand back and forth on the left arm in a sweeping motion. Repeat.

Creativity

When singing and signing songs there is lots of room for parental and toddler creativity and many children's songs are easily adaptable. You can take traditional rhymes and familiar songs in new directions. You can change a word here and there to fit in special areas of interest for you and your toddler. You can even rewrite all the words to create new songs.

For example, once you have learned the song "Stop, Look, and Listen," you can be creative and change the song to support the learning of animals. Simply change the words CAR, FIRE TRUCK, JET, and so on to words for animals like CAT, DOG, or BIRD.

Songs for You to Sing and Sign

Some of the Sign to Speak songs included here may be familiar to you and others may not. You can learn all the songs in the book on-line by visiting www.signtospeak.com and using the log-in access code STST109A. Remember that if you don't know the melody or are uncomfortable singing the song, you can just say it or chant it as you sign the words. As with the rhymes, we are offering you suggestions for key words. You can use all or just a few of them. You will also find additional signs you can add to each song later as well as tips to enhance your signing experience. Detailed information on each sign featured is found in the glossary.

If You're Happy and You Know It

Be sure to demonstrate the meaning of the feelings by the expressions on your face.

If you're HAPPY and you know it clap your hands. [*clap, clap*]
If you're HAPPY and you know it clap your hands. [*clap, clap*]
If you're HAPPY and you know it,
Then your FACE [*expression*] will surely show it,
If you're HAPPY and you know it clap your hands. [*clap, clap*]

If you're TIRED and you know it go to BED. [*snore*]
If you're TIRED and you know it go to BED. [*snore*]
If you're TIRED and you know it,
Then your FACE [*expression*] will surely show it,
If you're TIRED and you know it go to BED. [*snore*]

If you're SILLY and you know it LAUGH out loud. [*laugh*]
If you're SILLY and you know it LAUGH out loud. [*laugh*]
If you're SILLY and you know it,
Then your FACE [*expression*] will surely show it,
If you're SILLY and you know it LAUGH out loud. [*laugh*]

If you're ANGRY and you know it stomp your feet. [*stomp*]
If you're ANGRY and you know it stomp your feet. [*stomp*]
If you're ANGRY and you know it,
Then your FACE [*expression*] will surely show it,
If you're ANGRY and you know it stomp your feet. [*stomp*]

If you're HAPPY and you know it SIGN all four:
HAPPY, TIRED, SILLY, ANGRY. [with *expressions*]
If you're HAPPY and you know it SIGN all four:
HAPPY, TIRED, SILLY, ANGRY. [with *expressions*]
If you're HAPPY and you know it,
Then your FACE will surely show it,
If you're HAPPY and you know it SIGN all four:
HAPPY, TIRED, SILLY, ANGRY. [with *expressions*]

HAPPY   FACE   TIRED

BED   SILLY   LAUGH

ANGRY   SIGN

Stop, Look, and Listen

This song is designed to reinforce the learning of STOP, LOOK, and LISTEN, along with transportation words such as TRAIN, CAR, FIRE TRUCK, AIRPLANE, HELICOPTER, and MOTORCYCLE. It is ideal for using with children when you are out on a walk, crossing the street, or walking through a parking lot, and it often turns these activities into fun learning and behavior-shaping games.

STOP, LOOK, and LISTEN!
TRAIN is a coming, Oh YEAH.
TRAIN is a coming, Oh YEAH.
TRAIN is a coming, TRAIN is a coming,
TRAIN is a coming, Oh YEAH.
STOP, LOOK, and LISTEN!

CAR is a coming, Oh YEAH.
CAR is a coming, Oh YEAH.
CAR is a coming, CAR is a coming,
CAR is a coming, Oh YEAH.
STOP, LOOK, and LISTEN!

FIRE TRUCK'S a coming, Oh YEAH.
FIRE TRUCK'S a coming, Oh YEAH.
FIRE TRUCK'S a coming, FIRE TRUCK'S a coming,
FIRE TRUCK'S a coming, Oh YEAH.
STOP, LOOK, and LISTEN!

AIRPLANE'S a coming, Oh YEAH.
AIRPLANE'S a coming, Oh YEAH.
AIRPLANE'S a coming, AIRPLANE'S a coming,
AIRPLANE'S a coming, Oh YEAH.
STOP, LOOK, and LISTEN!

HELICOPTER'S coming, Oh YEAH.
HELICOPTER'S coming, Oh YEAH.
HELICOPTER'S coming, HELICOPTER'S coming,
HELICOPTER'S coming, Oh YEAH.
STOP, LOOK, and LISTEN!

MOTORCYCLE'S coming, Oh YEAH.
MOTORCYCLE'S coming, Oh YEAH.
MOTORCYCLE'S coming, MOTORCYCLE'S coming,
MOTORCYCLE'S coming, Oh YEAH.
STOP, LOOK, and LISTEN!

STOP   LOOK   LISTEN

TRAIN CAR FIRE TRUCK

AIRPLANE/JET HELICOPTER MOTORCYCLE YES/YEAH

One Little Kitty

Use the sign for the animal when you are making the sound it makes. You can also change the animals, and you could extend the song to 10 by adding numbers 6 to 10 and other animals mimicking their sounds and actions. Additional signs can be found in the glossary.

ONE little KITTY came out to PLAY.
ONE little KITTY had this to say,
Meow, Meow, Meow, Meow.
ONE little KITTY then WALKED away.

TWO little DUCKS came out to PLAY.
TWO little DUCKS had this to say,
Quack, Quack, Quack, Quack.
TWO little DUCKS then WADDLED away.

THREE little FROGS came out to PLAY.
THREE little FROGS had this to say,
Ribbit, Ribbit, Ribbit, Ribbit.
THREE little FROGS then HOPPED away.

FOUR little BIRDS came out to PLAY.
FOUR little BIRDS had this to say,
Tweet, Tweet, Tweet, Tweet.
FOUR little BIRDS then FLEW away.

FIVE little MONKEYS came out to PLAY.
FIVE little MONKEYS had this to say,
Ook, Ook, Ook, Ook.
FIVE little MONKEYS then RAN away.

ONE   TWO   THREE   FOUR   FIVE

CAT/KITTY   DUCK   FROG

BIRD   MONKEY

PLAY   WALK   WADDLE

HOP   FLEW   RUN

Old MacDonald

This traditional song supports the learning of signs for animals in conjunction with the spoken word and the sound the animal makes. You may find that signing E I E I O is difficult for very young fingers to accomplish so add them when you think your child is ready. You can be creative with this song by changing the animals you sing about. Use the sign for the animal when you are making its sound. This song is usually sung with each animal, and once introduced, each animal is repeated after the next animal throughout the rest of the song. You can add the letters E, I, and O to this song (found in the glossary).

OLD MacDonald had a FARM, E-I-E-I-O.
And on his FARM he had a COW, E-I-E-I-O.
With a MOO, MOO here and a MOO, MOO there.
Here a MOO, there a MOO, everywhere a MOO, MOO.
OLD MacDonald had a FARM, E-I-E-I-O.

Repeat the verse for other animals such as PIG, DUCK, SHEEP, and HORSE.

OLD   FARM

COW   PIG

DUCK   SHEEP   HORSE

The More We Get Together

This traditional song supports the learning of some useful signs such as MORE, PLAY, SING, MY, YOUR, and HAPPY. You can be creative by changing PLAY and SIGN with other action words like SING or DANCE. Add the sign for FRIEND later (found in the glossary).

The MORE we get TOGETHER, TOGETHER, TOGETHER,
The MORE we get TOGETHER, the HAPPIER we'll be.
Because MY friends are YOUR friends, and YOUR friends are MY friends,
The MORE we get TOGETHER, the HAPPIER we'll be.

The MORE we PLAY together, TOGETHER, TOGETHER,
The MORE we PLAY together, the HAPPIER we'll be.
Because MY friends are YOUR friends, and YOUR friends are MY friends,
The MORE we PLAY together, the HAPPIER we'll be.

The MORE we SIGN together, TOGETHER, TOGETHER,
The MORE we SIGN together, the HAPPIER we'll be.
Because MY friends are YOUR friends, and YOUR friends are MY friends,
The MORE we SIGN together, the HAPPIER we'll be.

MORE   TOGETHER   YOUR   MY

HAPPY   PLAY   SIGN

Jacob Wore a Red Hat

This fun song supports the learning of colors. You can easily be creative by changing the hat to another piece of clothing and inserting your child's and his friends' names for the ones used in this song.

Jacob wore a RED HAT, RED HAT, RED HAT.
Jacob wore a RED HAT, all day long.
Katelyn wore a BLUE HAT, BLUE HAT, BLUE HAT.
Katelyn wore a BLUE HAT, all day long.
Joey wore a YELLOW HAT, YELLOW HAT, YELLOW HAT.
Joey wore a YELLOW HAT, all day long.
Sarah wore an ORANGE HAT, ORANGE HAT, ORANGE HAT.
Sarah wore an ORANGE HAT, all day long.
Billy wore a GREEN HAT, GREEN HAT, GREEN HAT.
Billy wore a GREEN HAT, all day long.
Ali wore a RAINBOW HAT, RAINBOW HAT, RAINBOW HAT.
Ali wore a RAINBOW HAT, all day long.

HAT   RED   BLUE

YELLOW   ORANGE

GREEN   RAINBOW

Oh Where, Oh Where Has My Little Dog Gone?

The fun of this song is enhanced by looking around, as if you are really looking for something when you are signing WHERE. Be creative by substituting other animals for DOG, like CAT or HORSE (found in the glossary).

Oh WHERE, oh WHERE has my little DOG gone?
Oh WHERE, oh WHERE can he be?
With his EARS cut short and his TAIL cut long,
Oh WHERE, oh WHERE can he be?

WHERE   DOG

EAR   TAIL

Conclusion

Signing with songs and rhymes offers parents, teachers, and caregivers highly interactive, language-rich, and playful activities for their toddlers to support early learning. Simple rhymes, including Mother Goose Nursery Rhymes, are timeless favorites for use with small children, and by adding sign language, you are creating a way for your toddler to move and learn all at the same time. Signing with songs is another learning activity that involves the verbal, physical, and visual learning styles, as with rhymes, and then adds musical learning to the mix. All of these together strengthen memorization and recall abilities, giving toddlers a much larger collection of usable words that enables them to not only learn more but also support reading readiness.

Keep in mind that when rhyming and singing songs, you should keep the activity simple and use only a few signs. Add more signs as your toddler starts to use the beginning signs. Don't worry about your singing voice, as your toddler is more interested in the interaction. Be enthusiastic when you sing the songs and tell the rhymes. Show that you are excited to be involved with your toddler and you are enjoying the activity. Remember that toddlers love to repeat everything over and over so follow their lead and repeat or move on to other activities as they wish. Praise all efforts and try to use the signs at other times during your day.

Toddlers at Play Toolbox

Glossary of Signs

This glossary includes an alphabetical listing of all the signs mentioned in *Toddlers at Play.* You can use it for quick reference to recall any words that you have forgotten or you can look up words that are of particular interest to you and your toddler and then add them to your signing vocabulary.

Here are some basic tips to remember as you practice using new signs:

- Most signs are signed in an area from your shoulders to your waist and from side to side.
- Alphabet and number signs are signed near the shoulder of the hand you are using to sign.
- Use your dominant hand as your main signing hand. If you are left-handed, use your left hand; if you are right-handed, use your right hand.
- Use facial expressions to enhance the meaning of the words.

Basic Hand Information

Your hand

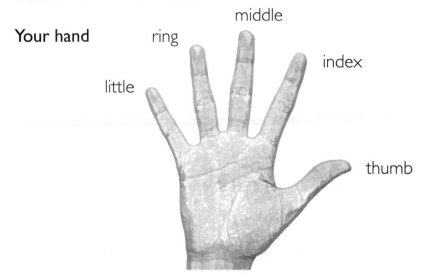

middle

ring

index

little

thumb

Types of hands

Flat hand

Spread flat with loose fingers

Claw hand

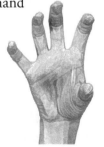

Palm in

Palm out

Palm facing to the side

Cupped hand

5 hand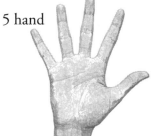

Numbers

1

2

3

4

5

6

7

8

9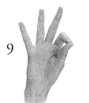

10

Alphabet

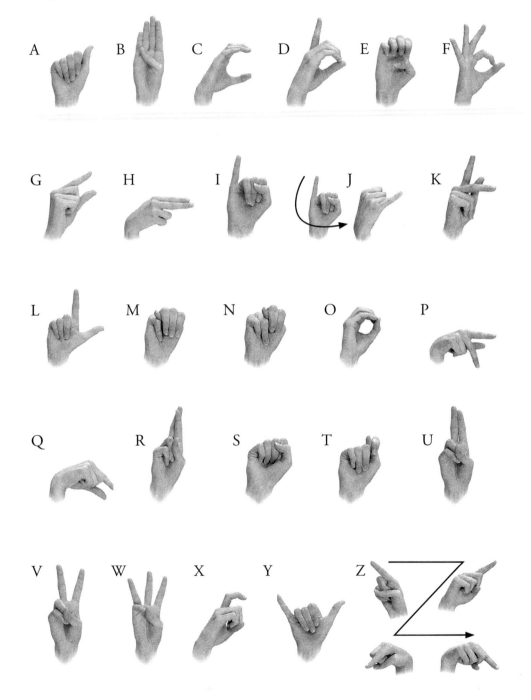

Glossary

Above

Hold both hands flat, palms down, with right hand on top of your left hand. Raise right hand up several inches in an arching motion.

Afraid / Frightened

Make the letter A with both hands and hold them at each side of your chest with palms facing in. With a quick motion, open up both your hands, with fingers pointing toward each other. Your facial expression should reflect being afraid.

Again

Hold both hands bent and palm up. Move your right hand up and over until the fingertips are touching the palm of your left hand.

Airplane   *See JET*

All Done / Finished

Hold up both hands with palms in, fingers at chest level, with palms flat and fingers loose. Then, in a quick motion, turn your palms so that they are facing out. Repeat.

All Gone

Make the letter O with both hands and place one under your chin and the other about midchest. Then move your hands downward while opening them up with your palms facing down.

Angry *See MAD*

Apple

Make the letter X with one hand and place the knuckle of the index finger near the side of your mouth and twist it downward twice.

Awake / Wake Up

Hold the index fingers and thumbs of both your hands together by the side of your closed eyes. Open your fingers as you open your eyes.

Baby

Fold your arms in front of yourself as if you are holding a baby, and rock them from side to side twice as if you are rocking a baby.

Ball

With your fingers spread and curved, tap the fingertips of both hands together at chest level. Repeat.

Banana

Hold one index finger up, palm forward; then with the other hand, pretend you are peeling a banana from the top of your raised index finger down. The first motion is near the back of the index finger, and the second motion is near the front.

Bath

Hold your fists, thumbs up, at the sides of your chest, then rub up and down repeatedly (as if you are washing your chest).

Bear / Teddy Bear

.Cross your arms at your chest and scratch your fingers up and down repeatedly.

Bed *See SLEEP*

Big

Make the letter L with both hands and hold them with your palms facing each other in front of your body. Then move them apart in an arch.

Bird / Hen / Chick

Hold your right hand by your mouth, with your index finger and thumb pointed out. Open and close these fingers, imitating the movement of a bird's beak.

Blanket

With both hands, imitate the movement of pulling a blanket up.

Blow

Hold your hand up, fingertips and thumb touching, in front of your mouth, with your palm facing forward. Then move it forward a little as you open it up and blow with your mouth.

Blue

Make the letter B with your right hand and then shake it (at the wrist) near the right side of your chest.

Boat

Cup your hands together, palms facing up, and move your hands forward in a bouncing motion (as if a boat was going over waves).

Book

Hold your flat hands together at chest level. Open your hands while keeping the little fingers touching (as if you are opening a book).

Bottle

Lay your left hand flat, palm up. Set your right hand on it as if you are holding a bottle, then lift it up, squeezing your hand together, representing how it narrows at the top.

Boy

Make a flattened letter C and hold it up near your forehead. Then close your fingers to your thumb, imitating the movement of grasping the bill of a cap.

Brother

Make the letter L with both hands, palms facing each other. Place your right hand with the thumb of the L touching your forehead. Hold the left hand down at chest level. Move your hand from your forehead downward until the little finger is resting just behind the thumb of your left hand.

Brush Teeth

With your index finger extended from a fist hand and held by your mouth, imitate the movement of brushing your teeth.

Bug

Make a fist and extend your thumb, index, and middle fingers. Touch your thumb to your nose and bend your index and middle fingers with a repeated movement.

Bunny *See RABBIT*

Can

Make the letter S with both hands and hold them, palms facing down, in front of your body. Move them downward a short distance. Repeat.

Car

Make the letter S with both hands and palms facing toward each other, held at your chest. Imitate the movement of holding a steering wheel and driving a car.

Careful

Make the letter K with both hands and hold them in front, one hand above the other. Tap the little finger of one hand on the index finger of the other.

Carrot

Make the letter S with one hand and hold it by your cheek and snap it as if you are biting off a piece of a carrot.

Cat / Kitty

Make the letter F using both hands, palms facing each other; hold them near the sides of your mouth, and pull outward as if you are tugging on the whiskers of a cat. Repeat.

Cereal / Porridge / Curds & Whey

Extend your index finger on your right hand. Place it on the left side of your face, then draw it to the right, under your mouth, wiggling your finger as you move it across your chin.

Chair / Tuffet

Make the letter U with both hands and palms facing down; place your right hand with curved fingers on top of the fingers of your left. Tap twice.

Change

Make the letter X with both hands, one on top of the other, with your palms facing each other. Twist your hands so that they switch position. The opposite hand is now on top.

Cheese

Hold both hands open, fingers slightly bent, left hand palm up and right hand palm down. Place the heel of your right hand against the heel of the other, and twist it forward and back repeatedly.

Chick *See BIRD*

Child

With a bent hand at your side, palm down, move it up and down as if you are touching the top of a child's head.

Chin

Using your index finger, point to your chin.

Close Eyes

Make the letter L with both hands turned and held up by your eyes; touch your index finger to your thumb while you close your eyes.

Clothes

With open hands, brush your thumbs down on each side of your chest. Repeat.

Coat

Make the letter Y with both hands. Hold them up near your shoulder and pull them inward to the middle of your chest. (like you are pulling on a coat).

Cold

Make the letter S with both hands and hold them at chest level, palms facing each other. Shake them from side to side with hunched shoulders (as if you are cold).

Come

Hold both fist hands with index fingers extended, palms up, extended in front of you. Then bring your fingers back and point at your chest.

Cookie

Hold your left hand flat, palm up. Curve the fingers of your right hand so your fingertips form a circle (as if holding on to the edges of a round cookie). Then touch your left palm twice, once directly on it and the second twisted slightly so it looks as if you are using a cookie cutter.

Cow

Make the letter Y with your hand. With your thumb on each side of your head, rotate your little fingers forward with a twist of your wrists (representing the horns on a cow).

Cracker

Hold your left arm bent and across your body. Make the letter A with your right hand, palm up; tap it near the elbow of your left arm.

Cry

Bring both extended index fingers up to your face, palms facing in, and then move them down your cheeks, alternating sides, as if tears are rolling down your cheeks.

Cup

Hold your left hand flat. Shape your right hand as if you are holding a cup, and then lift it. Repeat.

Daddy *See FATHER*

Dance

With your left hand flat, palm up, make the letter V with your right fist hand and point your fingertips toward the palm of your left hand. Then move it side to side (as if your fingers are dancing).

Diamond

Forming the letter D with your right hand, tap the tips of your finger twice.

Dog / Puppy

With a flat hand, tap the side of your hip. Then bring your hand up and snap your fingers.

Doll

Make the letter X with your right hand and brush the tip of your nose with the knuckle of your index finger. Repeat.

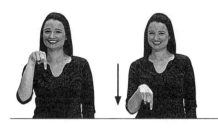

Down

With your index finger extended from a fist hand pointed down along the right side of your body, move your hand in a downward motion.

Dream

Make a fist with your index finger pointing out. Hold it next to your temple, palm down, then move it outward, bending your finger up and down to indicate that you are thinking.

Drink

Shape your hand as if you are holding a glass, then bring it up to your mouth and tip it toward you so that it looks as if you're drinking from that glass.

Duck

This sign is similar to BIRD. Hold out the index and middle fingers of one hand near your mouth, palm facing forward. Open and close them against your thumb. This looks like the wide bill of a duck.

Ear

Pinch your earlobe between your index finger and thumb and wiggle it.

Eat / Taste

Hold the thumb and fingertips of one hand together and bring your hand up to your mouth repeatedly (as if you are eating something).

Elephant

Beginning at your nose, move your flat hand, palm out, out and down, indicating the trunk of an elephant.

Face

With an extended index finger, draw a circle around your face.

Farm

Make the number 5 with your right hand; move the thumb of your right hand across your chin from the left side to the right.

Father / Daddy / Papa

Make the number 5 hand with one hand, and touch your thumb to your forehead. Repeat.

Feel / Feelings

Make the number 5 with a bent middle finger. With your palm facing in, touch your middle finger to the center of your chest, and move it upward.

Find

Hold your left hand flat, palm up. Make the number 5 with your right hand, palm down and above your left hand, extend your index finger and thumb onto the palm of your left hand, pinch them together, and move your right hand upward a short distance, forming the letter F.

Finished *See ALL DONE*

Fire Truck

Hold both hands up, fingers spread and slightly curved, and twist them side to side.

Fish

With a flat hand, mimic the movement of a fish as it swims.

Flew *See FLY*

Flower

Hold the fingertips and thumb of one hand together (as in the sign for EAT) and touch each side of your nose (as if you are smelling a flower).

Fly / Flew

Hold both flat hands up and by your side and flap them, as if you are flapping wings.

Friend

Extend bent index fingers from fists on both your hands, one palm up and the other palm down. Hook your index fingers together and then reverse their positions.

Frightened   *See AFRAID*

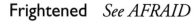

Frog

Make the letter S with one hand. Hold it under your chin, and then flick your index and middle fingers out. (This looks like the legs on a frog kicking out.) Repeat.

Game

With thumbs extended on fist hands, palms facing in, tap your knuckles together twice.

Gentle

Hold one hand flat, palm down. Then gently stroke the back of that hand.

Girl

Make the sign for the letter A, and hold your hand up to the side of your cheek, then move it down to your chin. Repeat.

Goldilocks   *Sign GIRL*

Good / Just Right

Hold your right hand flat, near your mouth, then move it down to your left hand, which is held with the palm up in front of you. Both palms will be facing up, with the back of your right hand on the palm of your left hand.

Good Morning

This is a two-part sign—GOOD and MORNING. Hold your left hand flat, palm up and extended. Hold your right flat hand, palm in at your chin, and move it downward, placing it palm up onto your left hand. Then extend your right flat hand palm up, bent at the elbow, away from your body. With your left arm positioned across your body with your flat hand, palm down, touching at the right elbow, raise your right hand up (as if the sun is rising).

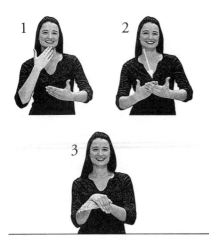

Good Night

This is a two-part sign—GOOD and NIGHT. Hold your left hand flat, palm up and extended. Hold your right flat hand, palm in at your chin, and move it downward, placing it palm up onto your left hand. Then extend your left hand across your body, palm down, and bring the fingers on your right hand, palm down, over the side of your left hand (as if the sun were setting).

Grandfather

Make the number 5 hand with one hand, and touch your thumb to your forehead. Then gesture outward, tracing two arches in the air.

Grandmother

Make the number 5 with one hand and touch your thumb at your chin. Then gesture outward, tracing two arches in the air.

Grapes

With your left hand flat, palm down, take your right claw hand and tap your fingertips on the back of your left hand several times, tapping a little farther away from the wrists to the fingers.

Green

Make the letter G with your right hand and hold it near your right side and shake it (at the wrist).

Happy

Hold your hands flat, palms in and thumbs up. Pat your chest in a circular motion. Use with a happy facial expression. Repeat.

Hat

Pat the top of your head twice with a flat hand.

Hear / Heard

Extend an index finger, and touch it to your ear.

Helicopter

This sign is made with a flat hand bouncing on an extended index finger or on the thumb of a hand made into the number 3.

Help

Hold one hand in a fist, thumb up, and the other hand flat, palm up. Lay your fist on top of your palm. Then lift both hands (as if one hand is helping the other). Use only your fist hand whenever you cannot make a two-handed sign.

Hen   *See BIRD*

High

Make the letter H with your right hand and move it from midchest to the right side of your head.

Hop

Hold the index finger of your right hand near the palm of your left flat hand. Lift up and bend your index finger with the motion of hopping.

Horse / Pony

Make a fist with your thumb out and your index and middle fingers up. Hold the thumb at the side of your head, and bend your index and middle fingers up and down twice (like the ears of a horse).

Hot

Hold your curved hand, fingers spread, near your mouth, palm in. Then, in a quick motion, pull your hand away, turning it outward and down a little (as if you're getting rid of something hot very fast).

House

With the fingertips of your hands touching, move your flat hands from the center of the "roof" out to the "walls" and then down (as if you are drawing the outline of the roof and walls of a house).

Hug

Make the letter S with fists crossed at the wrists, palms in and slightly off the chest. Pull them to your chest (as if you were hugging someone).

Hungry

Make the letter C, palm in, held at your chest. Move it down towards your stomach.

Hurt / Ouch

With both hands in fists, point index fingers toward each other and tap the fingertips together. Remember that this sign is directional. Sign it near the place where you hurt.

I / Me

Hold your fist up with your index finger out, and point to the middle of your chest.

I Love You *(shorthand, slang version)*

Hold your hand up near your shoulder, palm out, with your ring and middle fingers down, your index and little fingers up, and your thumb out. Keep this sign stationary; if you move it around, you'll be signing JET. Sometimes movement changes the meaning of a sign.

Inside

Touch all your fingertips to the thumb of your right hand. Then insert your right fingertips into a letter O, made with your left hand, palm in.

Jet / Airplane

Hold your right hand palm down with thumb, index, and little fingers held out. Then move it forward a short distance as if it's a jet plane.

Juice

Sign the letter J by your cheek. Then add the sign for DRINK by shaping your hand like a cup and tipping it towards your mouth.

Just Right *See GOOD*

Kiss

Touch your fingertips to your thumb on your right hand. Touch them to your face, near the right side of your mouth. Then open your hand and lay it on the side of your cheek.

Kitty *See CAT*

Lamb *See SHEEP*

Laugh

With a smile on your face make the letter L with both hands. Place index fingers near the sides of your mouth and pull your hands outward, pulling up slightly as if drawing a smile. Repeat.

Listen

Hold a cupped hand up near your ear (as if you are trying to listen).

Little
(as in small child) *See CHILD*

Little

(As in something small) Hold both hands open, facing each other and spread apart. Move your hands toward each other in a double movement, in front of your body.

Look

Make the letter V, palm down, your fingertips touching your cheek just under the eye. Then move your hand out in the direction of what you are looking at (as if your fingertips are an extension of your eyes).

Love

Make fists, crossed at the wrist, and hold them against your chest (as if you are holding something you love).

Mad / Angry

Hold your hand up with the fingertips curved, palm in front of your chin. Then squeeze your fingers together just a little and move your hand slightly toward your chin. Use an angry facial expression.

Mama *See MOTHER*

Me *See I*

Medicine

Hold your left hand flat, palm up. Make the number 5 with your right hand, bend the middle finger, place it on the palm of your left hand, then rock it side to side keeping the middle finger in place.

Merrily   *See HAPPY*

Milk

Squeeze your hand repeatedly (as if you are milking a cow).

Mommy   *See MOTHER*

Monkey

With both hands curved, palms in, scratch your sides twice in an upward movement (like a monkey scratching itself).

More

Hold the thumb and fingertips of both hands together (as you do with one hand for EAT) and then tap them together. Repeat.

Mother / Mommy / Mama

Make the number 5 with your hand and then tap your thumb on your chin. Repeat.

Motorcycle

Make the letter S with both hands, held up at your sides, palm down. Move your hands bending up and down at the wrists. Repeat.

My

Place your flat hand, palm in, against your chest.

Nice

Place your left hand flat palm up, right hand flat palm down, lay your right hand on top of the left and move it to your fingertips (as if you are wiping something off the left hand).

No

Extend your thumb, index, and middle fingers. Hold your index and middle fingers up and together, and close your fingers to your thumb. Move your hand slightly down.

Now

With palms facing up, bend both hands upward, hold them on each side of your body, and move them downward.

Old

Begin by making the letter C with your right hand near your chin. As you move your hand down (as if you are stroking a beard), squeeze your hand into a fist, changing it to an S hand.

Orange

Squeeze your hand into a fist in front of your mouth. This is the same sign for the color and the fruit.

Outside

Make the letter C with your left hand and hold it palm in. Place your right hand with loose fingers inside your left C hand. Then in a quick motion, pull your right hand up and out of the left, closing your fingertips to your thumb.

Owl

Make the letter O with both hands, hold them up by your eyes, and rotate.

Papa *See FATHER*

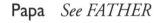

Pig

Hold the back of a flat hand under your chin. Bend your fingers at the knuckles, and move them up and down twice.

Pizza

Make the letter P with your right hand and draw the letter Z in the air.

Play

Make the letter Y with both hands, palms up, then twist them at the wrist to turn the palms up and down repeatedly.

Please

Rub a flat hand, palm in, in a circular motion on your chest.

Pony   *See HORSE*

Porridge   *See CEREAL*

Potty

Hold your right hand up forming the letter T and shake it side to side.

Puppy   *See DOG*

Purple

Make the letter P with your right hand and then shake it (at the wrist) near the right side of your chest.

Quiet

Hold flat hands up near your mouth, palms facing sideways, crossed at the wrists. Then, in a quick sweeping motion, move your hands down and apart, stopping at the waist with palms facing down.

Rabbit / Bunny

Cross both hands at the wrist with your index and middle fingers and thumb extended. Bend your fingers up and down with a double motion (like the ears on a bunny).

Rainbow

Make the number 4 with your right hand and move it from your left shoulder in an arch over to your right shoulder.

Ran   *See RUN*

Read

Hold your left hand up, your palm facing to the right. With the other hand, make the letter V, point the fingertips toward your left hand, and then move them from side to side and down (as if the right hand is reading words in a book).

Red

Extend your index finger from a fist and brush it downward, a short distance from your bottom lip twice.

Run / Ran

Make the letter L with both hands with hooked index fingers. Hook the index finger of your right hand around your left thumb. Wiggle your left index finger as you move both hands forward.

Run Away

Hold your right hand palm down and bent so that your index and middle fingers are extended and pointing downwards. Move your hand away with your fingers moving so that it looks like two legs running.

Sad

Hold your hands flat, fingers spread and palms facing in, at eye level and then move them down a little. Use with a sad facial expression.

Said *See SAY*

Sat *See SIT*

Say / Said

With your index finger out, touch it to your chin just below your lips, pointing to your mouth. Repeat.

See

Make the letter V with your right hand and hold it up near your eyes, palm in and move it away from your face a short distance.

Share

Both hands are flat with thumbs up. They are turned slightly away from your body. Place your right hand at the base of the thumb and index finger on the left hand, and move it back and forth twice.

Sheep / Lamb

Hold your left hand flat with your arm across your body. Make the letter V with your right hand, palm up, and open and close your extended fingers as you move them up your arm from the hand to the elbow (as if you are cutting the wool off a sheep).

Shirt

Pinch the upper right side of your shirt between the thumb and index finger of your right hand and pull. Repeat.

Shoe

Make the letter S with both hands, palms down and apart. Tap the sides of your fists together twice.

Sign

Make fists with both hands, extending the index fingers, and hold them pointing up. Then move your hands in large, alternating circles toward your chest.

Silly

Make the letter Y with one hand and hold it in front of your face. Twist at the wrist brushing your thumb across your nose. Repeat.

Sing / Song

Extend your left arm with a flat palm. Swing your flat right hand back and forth on the left arm in a sweeping motion. Repeat.

Sister

Make the letter L with both hands. Hold your left hand down and forward with your right thumb touching the side of your chin. Move your right hand down and lay its little finger just behind the thumb of your left hand (like BROTHER, except the sign begins at the chin).

Sit / Sat

Make the letter U with both hands, hook the fingers of your right hand and place them on top of the fingers of your left hand at chest level.

Sky

Move your right curved hand from over your head on the left side in a arch ending on your right side.

Sleep / Bed

With your head bent, close your eyes and rest your cheek on the palm of your flat hand (as if you are pretending to be asleep). You may also encounter this as a two-handed sign, with both hands held together and under a cheek. Either version is fine.

Smile

Hold flat hands slightly bent, with your fingertips near the sides of your mouth. Then move your hands up each side of your cheeks (as if you are drawing a smile).

Sock

Make fist hands; extend your index fingers, palms down, and then rub the sides of your fingers back and forth.

Song *See SING*

Spider

Make the number 4 with both hands, crossed at the wrists, palms down, and wiggle your fingers as if they were the legs of a spider walking.

Star

With extended index fingers on both hands, palms forward, brush the sides of your hands together in an alternating movement as your hands move upward.

Stop

Hold your left hand, palm up and extended. Hold your right flat hand facing in and chop it down quickly, laying it on top of your left hand. Use your facial expression to reinforce how strongly you mean STOP.

Story

Begin by making the letter C with both hands, one slightly palm up and the other slightly palm down. Touch your fingertips to your thumbs and pull your hands apart, ending near each shoulder. Repeat.

Tail

Hold your right hand in a fist with your index finger pointed out and slightly down. Hold your left hand in a fist, with your pointer finger pointing just behind the base of your right thumb. Wiggle your right hand (looks like a tail wagging).

Taste   *See EAT*

Teddy Bear   *See BEAR*

Thank You

Hold your right hand open and palm in, with your fingertips near your lips, and move it down and away, ending with your palm up.

Think

Double tap the side of your forehead with your pointed index finger.

Thirsty

Hold a fist hand with an extended index finger, palm in, near your neck. Bend your finger down the length of your neck.

Tired

Hold your hands flat, bent at the knuckles, with the palms facing in, fingertips touching at your shoulders. Roll your hands downward on your fingertips. Use with a tired facial expression and posture.

Together

Make the letter A with both hands, touch them together at your knuckles, and move them in a horizontal circle.

Toy

Make the letter T with both hands and hold them at your side, down and apart. Then twist them at your wrists. Repeat.

Train

Make the sign for the letter U with both hands, holding your palms down. Lay the fingers of your right hand on top of the fingers of your left. Then move the right-hand fingers back and forth on the left-hand fingers. Repeat.

Tuffet *See CHAIR*

Turtle

Make the letter A with your right hand turned to the side, cup your left hand over the top, and wiggle your thumb (as if the head of a turtle was extended from its shell and wiggling).

Twinkle

Make the number 5 with both hands and bend your middle fingers down. Hold your hands at midchest, palms facing to the side, and move one hand at a time up and at an angle while shaking. Repeat.

Up

Point your right index finger up and move it upward slightly.

Waddle

Hold flat hands, bent at the wrists, by your side. Alternately raise them up and down as you imitate the movement of waddling. Repeat.

Wait

Hold out both open hands, palms up, fingers bent, and wiggle your fingers. Repeat.

Wake Up *See AWAKE*

Walk

Hold both hands flat, palms down, in front of your body. Then move your fingertips and hands up and down by bending at the wrists and alternating the movement (as if your hands were walking).

Want

Make the number 5 with both hands, palms up, held in front of your body. Move them toward your body and curve your fingers in.

Wash

Make fists with both hands, right palm down and left palm up. Rub the right hand in a circular motion over the left hand. Repeat.

Water

Make the letter W with one hand and tap your index finger against your chin twice.

What

With your left flat hand facing right, draw a line with the index finger of your right hand across the fingers.

Where

Hold your index finger up and wave it from side to side.

Wolf

With a loose claw hand held palm in, up by your nose, move it out and close your fingertips (like the snout on a wolf).

Wonder

With your index finger, draw a circle near your forehead.

World

Make the letter W with both hands. Begin with hands touching at the wrists and then move the right hand in a circular motion out and around the left hand, ending where you started.

Yellow

Make the letter Y with your right hand, held at your side, and shake it at the wrist.

Yes / Yeah

Make the letter S with one hand, palm down. Then move it up and down at the wrist (like a head nodding yes).

You

Make a fist hand; point your index finger out and toward the person to whom you are talking.

Your

Hold a flat hand palm up near your chest and move it outward.

Resources

As you continue to sign with your child, you'll find these books and Web sites helpful.

Books

Apel, Kenn, and Julie J. Masterson. *Beyond Baby Talk: From Sounds to Sentences—A Parent's Complete Guide to Learning Language Development.* Roseville, CA: Prima Publishing, 2001.

Costello, Elaine. *Random House Webster's American Sign Language Dictionary.* New York: Random House, 1998.

Daniels, Marilyn. *Benedictine Roots in the Development of Deaf Education: Listening with the Heart.* Westport, CT: Bergin and Garvey, 1997.

Daniels, Marilyn. *Dancing with Words: Signing for Hearing Children's Literacy.* Westport, CT: Bergin and Garvey, 2001.

Fisch, Shalom M. *Children's Learning from Educational Television—Sesame Street and Beyond.* Mahwah, NJ: Erlbaum Associates, 2004.

Greenspan, Stanley I. *The Growth of the Mind and the Endangered Origins of Intelligence.* Cambridge, MA: Perseus Books, 1997.

Habermeyer, Sharlene. *Good Music Brighter Children.* Rocklin, CA: Prima Publishing, 1999.

Holt, John. *How Children Learn.* Cambridge, MA: Perseus Books, 1983.

Hughes, Fergus P. *Children, Play, and Development.* 3rd Ed. Boston, MA: Allyn and Bacon, 1999.

Leach, Penelope. *Your Baby and Child—From Birth to Age Five.* New York: Alfred A. Knopf, 1990.

On the Web

www.wesign.com
www.signtospeak.com
ASL Browser at http://commtechlab.msu.edu/sites/aslweb/browser.htm
www.Aslpro.com
www.Handspeak.com
www.dictionaryofsign.com
www.playalongsongs.com

Free Downloads and More

www.signtospeak.com
www.wesign.com

The Sign to Speak Toolbox and Handouts

Included in this Toolbox section are pages that you can use for quick reference.

1. 10 Signing Benefits for Toddlers
2. 12 Tips for Successful Signing with Toddlers
3. 10 Tips for Signing with Songs
4. Basic Colors
5. 12 Everyday Signs to Use with Toddlers

10 Signing Benefits for Toddlers

1. Increases toddlers' usable spoken, signed, and understood vocabulary

2. Helps toddlers understand and express their emotions

3. Reduces parent-toddler communication frustrations and eases the "terrible twos" and temper tantrums by providing toddlers with language skills they can use to express themselves

4. Supports brain development

5. Strengthens memory retention and recall

6. Provides an interactive bonding activity

7. Develops fine and gross motor skills

8. Builds self-confidence

9. Generates a real enthusiasm for learning

10. Promotes eye gaze, which strengthens literacy skills and increases academic success

12 Tips for Successful Signing with Toddlers

1. Focus on a few signs at a time, adding new signs as you become comfortable with signing.

2. Choose signs that reflect your signing goals along with signs that are of interest to your toddler.

3. Have your toddler's attention when signing.

4. Enunciate words clearly and sign ASL signs correctly.

5. Incorporate signing into your everyday life.

6. Consistently sign the word every time you say it.

7. Use exaggerated vocal and facial expressions.

8. Relate your signs to words and objects you are using.

9. Be creative about finding opportunities to sign.

10. Get everyone involved in signing.

11. Give lots of positive reinforcement.

12. Keep signing fun by using it with activities such as reading, singing, playing games, and more.

10 Tips for Signing with Songs

1. Keep your song activities simple. Sign just a few signs in the song and add more as you become more comfortable.

2. Choose short songs for toddlers as they work best.

3. Learn the signs you want to use and how to sing the song before engaging your toddler in the activity.

4. Teach your toddler the signs from the song before you sing it.

5. Sing and sign the song slowly at first. Pick up the tempo as your toddler's ability to participate grows.

6. Have your toddler's attention.

7. Be sure that your signs are clearly visible.

8. Use exaggerated facial expressions, voice, and signs.

9. Keep the activity fun and playful; be full of enthusiasm.

10. Praise all of your toddler's efforts.

Basic Colors

 *BLUE*

 *PURPLE*

 *GREEN*

 *ORANGE*

  *YELLOW*

  *RED*

  *RAINBOW*

12 Everyday Signs to Use with Toddlers

Photocopy and hang up for your quick signing reference.

Stop

Gentle

Help

Hurt

Change

Good

Share

Potty

Eat

Drink

Tired

I Love You

Notes

Chapter 1

1. Marilyn Daniels, *Dancing with Words: Signing for Hearing Children's Literacy* (Westport, CT: Bergin and Garvey, 2001): 77–84.
2. P. M. Prinz and E. A. Prinz, "Simultaneous Acquisition of ASL and Spoken English in a Hearing Child of a Deaf Mother and a Hearing Father: Phase I, Early Lexical Development," *Sign Language Studies* 25 (1978): 283–296.
3. D. Miller, "Signs a Helping Hand," *Charleston Gazette* 2000.
4. Miller, "Signs."
5. Howard Gardner, *The Unschooled Mind: How Children Think and How Schools Should Teach* (New York: Basic Books 1991).
6. Daniel Goleman, *Emotional Intelligence: Why It Can Matter More Than IQ* (New York: Bantam Books, 1995).

Chapter 2

1. Howard Gardner, *Intelligence Reframed: Multiple Intelligences for the 21st Century* (New York: Basic Books, 1999), 41.
2. Howard Gardner, *The Unschooled Mind: How Children Think and How Schools Should Teach* (New York: Basic Books, 1991), 45.
3. Daniel Goleman, *Emotional Intelligence: Why It Can Matter More Than IQ* (New York: Bantam Books, 1995), 35.
4. Goleman, *Emotional Intelligence,* 94.
5. Pat Wingert and Martha Brant, "Reading Your Baby's Mind," *Newsweek* August 15, 2005, 32–39.
6. Goleman, *Emotional Intelligence,* 273.
7. Goleman, *Emotional Intelligence,* 193.
8. Elizabeth Meins, "Mind-Reading Mums Boost Babies' Development," *New Scientist June 4,* 2005.
9. Yuichi Shoda, Walter Mischel, and P. Peake, "Predicting Adolescent Cognitive and Self-Regulatory Competencies from Preschool Delay of Gratification." *Developmental Psychology* 26 (1990): 978–986.
10. Marian Radke-Yarrow and Carolyn Zahn-Waxler, "Roots Motives and Patterns in Children's Prosocial Behavior," in *Development and Maintenance of Prosocial Behavior,* ed. Erwin Staub (New York: Plenum, 1984).
11. Goleman, *Emotional Intelligence,* 112.
12. P. Kolers, "Interlingual Word Associations," *Journal of Verbal Learning and Verbal Behavior* 2 (1963): 291–300.
13. Harry Hoemann, "Categorical Coding of Sign and English in Short Term Memory by Deaf and Hearing Subjects," in *Understanding Language through Sign Language Research,* ed. P. A. Siple (New York: Academic Press, 1978).
14. Harry Hoemann and T. Koenig, "Categorical Coding of Manual and English Alphabet Characters by Beginning Students of American Sign Language" *Sign Language Studies* 67 (1990): 175-181.

15. Erick Kandal, *In Search of Memory: The Emergence of a New Science of Mind* (New York: W. W. Norton, 2007).

16. David Eagleman, "Ten Unsolved Mysteries of the Brain," *Discover,* August 2007, 54–59.

17. Sharon Begley, *Train Your Mind, Change Your Brain* (New York: Ballantine Books, 2007).

18. William James, *Principles of Psychology* (New York: Holt, 1890).

19. Begley, *Train Your Mind.*

20. Lee Woodruff and Bob Woodruff, *In an Instant: A Family's Journey of Love and Healing* (New York: Random House, 2007): 91–92.

21. David Linden, *The Accidental Mind* (Cambridge, MA: Harvard University Press, 2007).

22. Begley, *Train Your Mind.*

23. Robertson Davies, *What's Bred in the Bone* (New York: Penguin Books, 1986).

24. Frank R. Wilson, *The Brain: How Its Use Shapes the Brain, Language, and Human Culture* (New York: Pantheon Books, 1998).

25. Wilson, *The Brain,* 188.

26. R. Restak, *The New Brain* (New York: Rodale/St. Martin's Press, 2003).

27. Restak, *The New Brain.*

28. Burton White, *The First Three Years of Life* (New York: Simon & Schuster, 2005).

29. B. Lohmann, "A Time to Speak," *Richmond Times-Dispatch,* D1, D3 (1999).

30. Ibid.

Chapter 3

1. William C. Stokoe, "The Once New Field: Sign Language Research or Breaking Sod in the Back Forty," *Sign Language Studies,* 93 (1996): 388.

Bibliography

Begley, Sharon. *Train Your Mind, Change Your Brain.* New York: Ballantine Books, 2007.

Daniels, Marilyn. *Dancing with Words: Signing for Hearing Children's Literacy.* Westport, CT: Bergin and Garvey, 2001.

Davies, Roberson. *What's Bred in the Bone.* New York: Penguin Books, 1986.

Eagleman, David. "Ten Unsolved Mysteries of the Brain." *Discover,* August 2007.

Gardner, Howard. *Intelligence Reframed.* New York: Basic Books, 1999.

Gardner, Howard. *The Unschooled Mind: How Children Think and How Schools Should Teach.* New York: Basic Books, 1991.

Goleman, Daniel. *Emotional Intelligence: Why It Can Matter More Than IQ.* New York: Bantam Books, 1995.

Groggin, J., and D. Wickens. "Proactive Interference and Language Change in Short-Term Memory." *Journal of Verbal Learning and Verbal Behavior,* 10 (1971).

Hoemann, H. "Categorical Coding of Sign and English in Short Term Memory by Deaf and Hearing Subjects." In *Understanding Language Through Sign Language Research,* edited by P. A. Siple New York: Academic Press, 1978.

Hoemann, H., and T. Koenig. "Categorical Coding of Manual and English Alphabet Characters by Beginning Students of American Sign Language," *Sign Language Studies* 67 (1990).

Holt, John. *How Children Learn.* Rev. ed. Cambridge, MA: Perseus Books, 1983.

Hughes, Fergus P. *Children, Play, and Development.* 3rd ed. Boston, MA: Allyn & Bacon, 1995.

James, William. *Principles of Psychology.* New York: Holt, 1890.

Kandal, Erick. *In Search of Memory: The Emergence of a New Science of Mind.* New York: W. W. Norton, 2007.

Kolers, P. "Interlingual Word Associations." *Journal of Verbal Learning and Verbal Behavior* 2 (1963).

Linden, David. *The Accidental Mind.* Cambridge, MA: Harvard University Press, 2007.

Lohmann, B. "A Time to Speak." *Richmond Times-Dispatch,* D1, D3, (April 1999).

Meins, E. "Mind-Reading Mums Boost Babies' Development." *New Scientist* (June 2005).

Radke-Yarrow, Marian, and Carolyn Zahn-Waxler. "Roots Motives and Patterns in Children's Prosocial Behavior." In *Development and Maintenance of Prosocial Behavior,* editor Erwin Staub. New York: Plenum, 1984.

Restak, Richard. *The Naked Brain.* New York: Harmony Books, 2006.

Restak, Richard. *The New Brain.* New York: Rodale/St. Martin's Press, 2003.

Shoda, Yuichi, Walter Mischel, and P. Peake. "Predicting Adolescent Cognitive and Self-Regulatory Competencies from Preschool Delay of Gratification." *Developmental Psychology,* 26 (6), 1990.

White, Burton. *The First Three Years of Life.* New York: Simon & Schuster, 2005.

Wilson, Frank R. *The Brain: How Its Use Shapes the Brain, Language, and Human Culture.* New York: Pantheon Books, 1998.

Wingert, Pat, and Martha Brant. "Reading Your Baby's Mind." *Newsweek* (August 15, 2005).

Woodruff, Lee. and Bob Woodruff. *In an Instant: A Family's Journey of Love and Healing.* New York: Random House, 2007.

The following are all studies that demonstrate increased vocabulary growth for hearing children through the use of sign.

Daniels, M. "ASL as a Factor in Acquiring English." *Sign Language Studies,* 78 (1993).

Daniels, M. "The Effect of Sign Language on Hearing Children's Language Development." *Communication Education,* 43 (1994a).

Daniels, M. "Words More Powerful Than Sound." *Sign Language Studies,* 83 (1994b).

Daniels, M. "Bilingual, Bimodal Education for Hearing Kindergarten Students." *Sign Language Studies,* 90 (1996a).

Daniels, M. "Seeing Language: The Effect Over Time of Sign Language on Vocabulary Development in Early Childhood Education." *Child Study Journal,* 26 (3) (1996b).

Daniels, M. "Teacher Enrichment of Pre-kindergarten Curriculum with Sign Language." *Journal of Research in Childhood Education,* 12 (1) (1997).

Daniels, M. "Sign Language Advantage." *Sign Language Studies* 2, no. 1 (2001a).

Daniels, M. "Sign Education: A Communication Tool for Young Learners." *Speech Communication Association of Pennsylvania Annual* 57 (2001b).

Daniels, M. "Reading Signs: A Way to Promote Childhood Literacy." *Communication Teacher* 16, no. 2 (2002).

Daniels, M. "Using a Signed Language as a Second Language for Kindergarten Students." *Child Study Journal* 3, no. 1 (2003).

Daniels, M. "American Sign Language as a Second Language for Hearing Kindergarten Students." *Communication Education.* In press.

Daniels, M. "The Silent Signs of Learning: ASL in a Special Needs Class." *Child Study Journal.* In press.

The following is the only study that demonstrates heightened spelling performance.

Daniels, M. "Relationship Between the Use of American Sign Language and Students' Self-esteem and Spelling Performance in a Learning Support Class." *Qualitative Research Reports in Communication.* In press.

Index

About the Authors

Dr. Marilyn Daniels

Since the 1990s, Dr. Marilyn Daniels has been one of the premier authors and researchers on the use of American Sign Language with hearing children. She has been quoted extensively in many publications and has appeared on radio and television for over 20 years. She is a professor of communication arts and sciences at Pennsylvania State University.

Dr. Marilyn Daniels

Her first study, "ASL as a Factor in Acquiring English," was published in *Sign Language Studies* in 1993. Since then she has published 19 additional research studies and two books on this subject, including her widely quoted book *Dancing with Words: Signing for Hearing Children's Literacy.* She has been in numerous magazines and newspapers in the United States, Canada, and England. Marilyn also lectures and presents workshops to help parents, teachers, and other caregivers learn how to effectively use sign language with hearing children.

Her research has taken place in a variety of locations in the United States, from Vermont to California. In addition, she has been actively involved in several sign language projects throughout the world. Recently, she introduced the Canadian Association for the Deaf and Hard of Hearing to the ASL literacy process that she is engaged in with hearing children in the United States.

She has served as a consultant to several ongoing sign language projects in the United Kingdom. In these endeavors, British Sign Language is being used to improve learning with young students. In addition, she taught summer courses at Nagoya University in Nagoya, Japan, to teachers of English as a second language.

Ken Frawley

Ken Frawley graduated from California State University, Fullerton with a bachelor's degree in liberal studies, intending to become an elementary school teacher. Instead, he began to perform, often with his wife, Georgia, at children's and family concerts at schools, libraries, and community events throughout Southern California. He has written over 200 children's songs used around the country and is an award-winning producer of video products for children. He has taught thousands of parents and teachers across the country how to incorporate singing and signing into the lives of children, from birth to elementary school. He has performed his play-along and signing songs with hundreds of thousands of children for many years. In addition, he coproduced the multiple award-winning *Say, Sing and Sign* video and the We Sign DVD series.

He and Georgia experienced the benefits of signing with their own children in the 1980s. They used sign not only to enhance communication, but as part of songs and

Ken and Georgia Frawley

games that provided for fun family interaction while supporting early learning of educational concepts. They later included signing activities in their children's concerts and shows. From these experiences they developed programs for using sign with all hearing children, from babies to elementary school ages, and have taught their concepts and techniques to parents and educators across the country.

Georgia Frawley

Georgia Frawley, MA, began working as a dorm counselor at the California School for the Deaf in Riverside, California, while she was finishing her teaching credential in physical education and home economics from California State Polytechnic University, Pomona. By the end of her first day of work, the children had taught her over 30 signs.

When she married Ken and they had a daughter, Coreen, signing with her was second nature to Georgia. As she talked, Georgia also signed the same words she had learned to use with the children from the School for the Deaf. It seemed to her that she was supporting language growth by making words visual for her young child.

She has been teaching Child Development, Parenting, and Marriage and Family classes for over 30 years. While developing and running her on-campus day-care center, she received a masters degree in counseling, which she used to help the young parents at her high school. She has taught thousands of students and parents about the benefits of sign language and how to use signing effectively with young children.

About Production Associates

Production Associates has become a leader in producing quality educational video and DVD products for children from birth through elementary school. Since the early 1990s it has developed audio and video titles that have been sold across the United States. Its projects have included pilots for television, including a Russian language children's show, children's exercise videos, and phonemic awareness products. Hundreds of the songs it has produced for children are available on iTunes.

For over 15 years, the products developed by Production Associates have been highly acclaimed by parents, teachers, caregivers, and other early childhood professionals. The company has received over 50 national awards for its children's and family products.

Production Associates' first collection of sign language products was called Say, Sing and Sign, later to become the We Sign series. Since the beginning, each product and every song has been selected to support communication, learning, and language development; enhance vocabulary; and, above all, provide adults and children with fun, playful, and bonding activities.

The We Sign series has always featured American Sign Language. ASL is one of the most common languages in the country, and because of its movement and visual nature, it provides a wonderful way for children to be involved in their learning. We Sign uses an official language rather than made-up signs or gestures because ASL offers the structure and vocabulary of a language and hearing children receive many benefits through the use of signing.

Production Associates has sought not only to create a greater awareness regarding the use of signing with hearing children but also to develop signing activities that engage children. One of its goals has been to produce television products that create doers, not just viewers. The We Sign series encourages children to follow along, sing along, and sign along. Another goal is to promote signing to parents, teachers, and caregivers as a way to create playful learning and bonding interaction.

Now with the addition of the Sign to Speak books to the We Sign family, Production Associates is seeking to help parents, teachers, and other adults to become more proficient with signing, as well as to become educated about the science behind signing success. All these efforts are geared toward allowing children to get a "Jump Start on Smart," getting them started in school with a language-rich foundation that will help them succeed, increase their confidence, and develop an interest in learning that will last a lifetime.

Products

Babies, Toddlers, Preschoolers, and Elementary School Children

The We Sign Early Learning and Communication collection of DVDs features American Sign Language, instruction, and songs. These products are ideal for parents, teachers, and caregivers to use for interactive activities throughout the day. These products are especially useful with babies, toddlers, and preschoolers.

Babies and Toddlers—A comprehensive program that provides demonstrations, information, and instruction for parents on using sign language with babies and toddlers. It contains easy-to-follow practical advice, useful beginning signs, 12 baby songs, and a video dictionary of over 230 words to use with children.

Play Time—Fun interactive songs, featuring the We Sign Kids, for young children and their parents, families, and caregivers to sing and sign together. Songs included are "The Wheels on the Bus," "One Little Kitty," "This is the Way We Wash Our Hands," "If You're Happy and You Know It," "A Really Good Treat," "Stop, Look, and Listen," "Jacob Wore a Red Hat," "Jumping," and "Raindrops."

Fun Time—Energetic songs, featuring the We Sign Kids, that involve children and families in singing and signing activities. Songs included are "Five Little Monkeys," "I See, I Hear, I Smell," "Old MacDonald," "Little Miss Muffet," "I'm Gonna Play," "There's a Little Song a Singing," "If I Were a Little Fish," "Mama I'm Readin'," "The More We Get Together," "Oh Where, Oh Where," and "Row, Row, Row Your Boat."

Special features include Spanish language tracks, closed captioning, subtitles, and a song jukebox.

Special features include We Sign Kids track, instructor track, Spanish language track, subtitles, closed captioning, and a song jukebox.

Preschool and Elementary Core Educational Support

A B C—Songs included are the "ABC Song," "ABC Object Song," and "S M I L E." Ideal for letter and sound recognition and spelling fun.

Numbers—Songs included are "One, Two, Buckle My Shoe," "The Number Song," "Ten to One Hundred," "Numbers and Things," "One Little Bird," and "One Fuzzy Caterpillar." An ideal way to learn numbers from 1 to 100 along with lots of vocabulary.

Colors—Songs included are "The Color Song," "Mixing All My Colors," "Let My Colors Flow," "The Snowman's Hat," and "Colors and Things." Learning about colors with signed songs is fun.

Rhymes—Songs included are "Mary Had a Little Lamb," "Twinkle, Twinkle Little Star," "Old Mother Hubbard," "It's Raining, It's Pouring," "Humpty Dumpty," "Rock-A-Bye Baby," "Little Bo Peep," "Wee Willie Winkie," "Little Jack Horner," and "Three Blind Mice." Children learn these classic rhymes as they sing and sign along.

Animals—Songs included are "Oh Where, Oh Where Has My Little Dog Gone," "Itsy Bitsy Spider," "Bat, Bat," "The Bear Went Over the Mountain," "Croak, Said the Toad," "Animal Parade," "Froggie Went A-Courtin'," and "Animal Alphabet." Playful animal songs for vocabulary building.

Additional We Sign Products

Classroom Favorites—Songs included are "Bingo," "Twinkle, Twinkle Little Star," "I Saw a Ship A-Sailing," "Earth, Earth, Earth," "Home on the Range," "This is the Way We Wash Our Hands," "Jingle Bells," "One Little," and "There Was an Old Woman." Comes with We Sign Kids track, Spanish language track, subtitles, and closed captioning.

More Animals—Songs included are "Animals Live All Around the World," "Thinking of an Animal," "They Call Home," and "Walking Through the Forest." Elementary children learn signs for animals along with lots of vocabulary. Comes with We Sign Kids track, Spanish language track, subtitles, and closed captioning.

Santa's Favorite Christmas Songs—Songs included are "Jingle Bells," "O Christmas Tree," "Up on the House Top," "Jolly Old St. Nicholas," "There Is Snow on the Mountain," "The Twelve Days of Christmas," and "We Wish You a Merry Christmas." Great songs for all ages.

Christmas Carols—Christmas carols included are "Silent Night," "Away in a Manger," "O Little Town of Bethlehem," "What Child Is This?" "Joy to the World," "God Rest Ye Merry Gentleman," and "O Come, All Ye Faithful." All ages love to sing and sign along to these classic carols.

American Patriotic Songs—Songs included are "Yankee Doodle," "America," "Grand Old Flag," "America the Beautiful," "Battle Hymn of the Republic," "Yankee Doodle Boy," "God Bless America," and "The Star Spangled Banner." Also featured on this DVD is the Pledge of Allegiance.

Books

Sign to Speak: Babies Can Talk—Signs and signing information designed to help parents and caregivers sign with babies.

Sign to Speak On-Line

Free on-line support is available with your book. Simply go to http://www.signtospeak.com and log in with the code STST109A to access a variety of additional resources.

FREE On-Line Music Downloads

Use your log-in code to listen to and download all the songs found in this book. Play them at home, in the car, or anywhere else you would like. Sing the melodies with your baby as often as you can.

FREE On-Line Video Demonstrations

- Signing music videos of all the songs in this book
- A signing video dictionary of all the signs featured

Simply use your log-in code to watch and learn from our video presentations. Discover how to sing and sign each of the songs and watch how any sign you are interested in is formed.

FREE On-Line Sheet Music Downloads

If you would like the sheet music so you can learn to sing and play the songs found in this book, just use your log-in code and download the music.

FREE On-Line Journal Page Samples

If you would like some ideas for your journal pages, we have provided several samples for you to use on our Web site. (You can download the pages with your log-in code.)